InTentional
InTERRUPTION

InTentional InTerruption

Breaking Down Learning Barriers to Transform Professional Practice

STEVEN KATZ
LISA AIN DACK

CORWIN
A SAGE Company

CORWIN
A SAGE Company

FOR INFORMATION:

Corwin
A SAGE Company
2455 Teller Road
Thousand Oaks, California 91320
(800) 233-9936
www.corwin.com

SAGE Publications Ltd.
1 Oliver's Yard
55 City Road
London, EC1Y 1SP
United Kingdom

SAGE Publications India Pvt. Ltd.
B 1/I 1 Mohan Cooperative Industrial Area
Mathura Road, New Delhi 110 044
India

SAGE Publications Asia-Pacific Pte. Ltd.
3 Church Street
#10–04 Samsung Hub
Singapore 049483

Acquisitions Editor: Debra Stollenwerk
Associate Editor: Desirée A. Bartlett
Editorial Assistant: Kimberly Greenberg
Permissions Editor: Adele Hutchinson
Project Editor: Amy Schroller
Copy Editor: Lana Todorovic-Arndt
Typesetter: Hurix Systems Pvt. Ltd
Proofreader: Charlotte J. Waisner
Indexer: Maria Sosnowski
Cover Designer: Bryan Fishman

Printed in the United States of America.

Library of Congress Cataloging-in-Publication Data

Katz, Steven, Ph.D.
Intentional interruption : breaking down learning barriers to transform professional practice / Steven Katz, Lisa A. Dack.

p. cm.
Includes bibliographical references and index.

ISBN 978-1-4129-9879-6 (pbk.)

1. Teachers—In-service training.
2. Professional learning communities.
I. Dack, Lisa A. II. Title.

LB1731.K34 2013

370.71'1—dc23

2012024333

This book is printed on acid-free paper.

SUSTAINABLE FORESTRY INITIATIVE
Certified Chain of Custody
Promoting Sustainable Forestry
www.sfiprogram.org
SFI-01268
SFI label applies to text stock

13 14 15 16 10 9 8 7 6 5 4

Contents

Preface

The Rationale

Professional learning is the cornerstone of many (if not most) school improvement efforts. The basic idea is that student learning, engagement, and success are dependent on high-quality practices in classrooms and schools. And high-quality practice emerges from meaningful professional learning. That said, despite best intentions, significant research has found that professional learning is often about activity rather than about learning. And if it's not about learning, then it is unlikely to have an impact on practice in a way that will lead to real and sustained improvements in schools. The key question, then, is what does it mean for professional learning efforts in schools and districts to really be about the kind of learning that truly improves practice?

The Focus

This book takes up that question. In essence, what does it mean to truly leverage the *learning* in professional learning? We have set the bar high in defining "learning" and use a strict, psychological definition of the term. Learning is a *permanent* change in thinking or behavior. When this permanence criterion is included in the definition of learning, it becomes easier to understand why typical professional development is often less about learning and more about activity. Real new learning is hard work. It is about people thinking, knowing, and understanding differently than they did before. Research has shown that this is very difficult because human beings are not naturally inclined to make these kinds of changes. Simply put, and contrary to conventional wisdom, our minds tend to get in the way. There is a range of "cognitive biases" that work to impede new learning—things that our minds do that get in the way of changing what we think, know, and understand.

Getting to real learning requires disrupting our natural propensity to avoid it. This is challenging and requires intentional facilitation of a particular sort—what we call *intentional interruption*. It's about an intentional interruption of the subtle cognitive and affective supports that work to preserve the status quo of thinking, knowing, and doing and that impede new learning. This book will outline what it means to intentionally interrupt the status quo of professional learning in order to enable real new learning that takes the form of permanent changes in thinking and practice.

Organization

This book is organized into six chapters: In Chapter 1, "From Activity to Learning," we provide an overview of our research-based theoretical model, which shows why professional learning is so important, as well as introduce our notion of facilitation as intentional interruption. In Chapter 2, "The (Very) Hard Work of Learning," we take a step back and examine in depth what learning is from a psychological perspective (a permanent change in thinking or behavior) and why it is so difficult to make it happen. In Chapter 3, "The Problem With Professional Learning," we describe how educators typically try to enable learning—through professional development activities—and why this is often problematic from a true learning orientation. In Chapter 4, "How Do Focus, Collaborative Inquiry, and Instructional Leadership Enable Learning?" we look at how professional learning that does have the potential to impact on teacher practice and student achievement occurs, specifically examining how it is enabled through focus, collaborative inquiry that challenges thinking and practice, and instructional leadership. In Chapter 5, "The Barriers: How Our Minds Get in the Way," we describe the psychological biases that interfere with professional learning and get in the way of putting the enablers (focus, collaborative inquiry, and instructional leadership) into place. These psychological biases are the barriers to real learning that need to be interrupted. In Chapter 6, "Intentional Interruption," we look carefully at the notion of interrupting the barriers to learning. Specially, we explore strategies and methodologies for intentionally interrupting the barriers described in Chapter 5 to ensure that focus, collaborative inquiry, and instructional leadership unfold in a way that truly enables learning.

Reading and Using This Book

This book is for anyone who has a stake in supporting the kind of professional learning that truly impacts on student achievement. This includes school, district, and legislative leaders who have responsibility for promoting professional learning and professional development. It also includes teachers, who are responsible for facilitating their own professional learning, as well as that of their colleagues. Wherever possible, we provide concrete, school-based illustrations of the ideas being described, with various roles reflected therein. These examples are drawn from real practice and come from our own work and experience in facilitating and researching professional learning in many school districts over the last decade. The book can be read straight through, or it can be a resource for learning and conversation among school and district teams. Each chapter finishes with a section called "Time for Reflection," which includes a number of reflection questions relating to major ideas in the chapter. These questions are designed to help readers digest and personalize the content of the chapters and can be considered either individually or in groups.

Acknowledgments

This book is the product of a continuing development and research agenda and couldn't have been possible without a range of partners in the field who, like us, were and are committed to an iterative cycle of trying, learning, and refining. In particular, our partnerships with the District School Board of Niagara (DSBN) and the Hamilton-Wentworth District School Board (HWDSB) have been invaluable. Leaders and practitioners at all levels of these systems have worked with us as we have continued to refine key ideas and practices over several years in environments that have valued the transparency of learning in the focused pursuit of student achievement. And we have seen the results. Key system leaders have found ways to bring us into their professional learning arenas and allowed us to be a part of them over multiple years as we worked to learn and build capacity together. This is what job-embedded learning really means, and we thank all of them very much. Of course, we would be nowhere without all of the administrators, consultants, coordinators, and teachers in the many school districts in which we work, who have invited us to their meetings and into their schools and classrooms. You know who you are; we are most grateful to you. Finally, to our friend and colleague, Lorna Earl, we thank you for your ongoing role as critical friend and conversation partner, as well as for your careful reading and suggestions on earlier drafts of this book that have helped to make it better.

Publisher's Acknowledgments

Corwin gratefully acknowledges the contributions of the following reviewers:

Lois Easton
Educational Consultant
Tucson, AZ

Mag Gardner
Superintendent of Student Achievement
Hamilton-Wentworth District School Board
Hamilton, ON, Canada

Glen Ishiwata
Superintendent (Retired)
Moreland School District
San Jose, CA

Terry Morganti-Fisher
Consultant
Learning Forward, QLD Learning
Austin, TX

Patricia W. Newhall
Associate Director
Landmark School Outreach Program
Prides Crossing, MA

Melanie Sendzik
Principal
District School Board of Niagara
St. Catharines, ON, Canada

About the Authors

Steven Katz is a director with the research and evaluation firm Aporia Consulting Ltd. and a permanent faculty member in Human Development and Applied Psychology at the Ontario Institute for Studies in Education of the University of Toronto (OISE, UT). He is an associate member of the School of Graduate Studies and is the coordinator of the Psychology of Learning and Development Initial Teacher Education program component.

Katz has a doctorate in human development and applied psychology, with a specialization in applied cognitive science. His areas of expertise include cognition and learning, teacher education, networked learning communities, and the design of data-driven systems for organizational accountability, planning, and improvement. He has received the Governor General's medal for excellence in his field and has been involved in research and evaluation, professional development, and consulting with a host of educational organizations around the world.

Lisa Ain Dack is a senior associate at Aporia Consulting Ltd. and an instructor of developmental and educational psychology in the Initial Teacher Education program throughout the University of Toronto. Lisa has a doctorate in developmental psychology and education from the Ontario Institute for Studies in Education of the University of Toronto (OISE, UT), with a collaborative degree in developmental science. Lisa leads numerous research projects investigating within-school professional learning communities and cross-school networked learning communities and has been involved in many research projects on assessment and evaluation. She also undertakes program evaluations at both the primary and secondary levels. In addition, Lisa leads workshops for administrators and teachers throughout Ontario on within-school professional learning communities and cross-school networked learning communities, as well as on data-driven decision making.

1

From Activity to Learning

Introduction

David is principal of Greenway School, a mid-size junior/intermediate school with approximately four hundred students and twenty teaching staff. His school is average when it comes to students' large-scale assessment results, with the results in numeracy slightly higher than in literacy. For the past year, David has been trying to work with his staff through their professional learning community (PLC) to raise student achievement, but he sometimes feels that they are going around in circles. For the most part, the teachers are keen to participate, but there is little agreement about the purpose of their PLC, and the content that they discuss at their meetings seems to change frequently, depending on what's going on around them at the time. The atmosphere is almost always nice and friendly, and someone usually brings a snack to share. There are currently two district initiatives that the school is involved in, one around a teaching and learning inquiry cycle and the other around increasing school safety, so the group takes a portion of each meeting to work on one of these. A few months ago, one of the teachers suggested doing a book study on a new, popular book about student motivation, so David bought each teacher a copy, and they discussed it for a few meetings. A month later, the vice principal went to a conference on numeracy, and she came back and presented to the staff about what she had learned. And just last week, another teacher suggested that, at the next PLC meeting, they meet in small groups to discuss how they are going to approach the upcoming report cards.

David thinks that these are all good ideas and is pleased that most of the teachers in the school are motivated to participate in the PLC. He wants to respect the ideas that they have and thinks it's important for the teachers to feel ownership over what they are learning, so he tends to embrace any suggestions that come up. But he does worry that the PLC is a bit disorganized and chaotic and wonders how it could possibly be having the impact on students that he intended. He worries that they are moving from activity to activity way too quickly. It seems that any time the group is on the brink of figuring something out, someone suggests a new idea for an activity, and they move on. He also worries about the behavior of his staff even within the activities they're doing. The teachers seem to tiptoe around one another and avoid sharing their honest thoughts about one another's ideas and practices. They seem not to know how to ask each other questions or how to provide feedback that includes any sort of challenge, and so their comments to one another tend to only include a kind of superficial affirmation, such as "sounds great." David knows enough about effective PLCs to wonder if this is problematic, but he has no idea what to do about it. He knows that the teachers are working very hard and are very busy, so he worries he'll discourage them if he interferes, but he's not sure if the PLC is actually making any difference. He frequently thinks about the fact that PLC stands for professional *learning* community and wonders if there's really any learning going on at all.

This scenario is one that we have encountered many times in slightly different forms, and it describes what we see as the major challenge of professional learning in schools and districts—that it is often more about activity than it is about learning. In this book, we take up this challenge by focusing on what it means to facilitate true professional learning—the kind that has an impact on classroom practice and on student achievement. This book is about why the diffused and unfocused professional learning that the Greenway teachers are involved in tends not to be impactful and what it means for professional learning to truly be about *learning*. And it is about why this kind of learning is so difficult and what it looks like to facilitate professional learning that results in deep and permanent changes.

Most schools in this day and age have some kind of professional learning agenda, and many schools have professional learning communities that look a lot like Greenway's. As you can see in this example, there is a lot of work happening at Greenway. Teachers at

Greenway are likely very busy and very tired, and they likely believe that their PLC is doing excellent work. You will see that our concern in this book is not with how to encourage people to do professional learning work; rather, it is with encouraging people to do the *right* work. And from our perspective, it is likely that Greenway's PLC is not doing the *right work* because, despite the fact that it's called a professional learning community, there is actually not that much learning going on, at least not the kind that will change anyone's thinking or practices.

As we will articulate throughout this book (particularly in the following chapter), we take a stringent view of what constitutes learning, and we define it as a *permanent* change in thinking or behavior. We will show that this kind of learning is very difficult to attain and that there are a number of barriers that stand in the way of it happening. Although Greenway's teachers are certainly working hard and likely believe that they are doing the right kind of work, the true test of their learning is whether it results in a change in their thinking and/or practices that make a significant difference for the students that they teach.

In the work that we do with schools, we frequently talk to teachers and administrators about the barriers that get in the way of making their professional learning efforts truly effective. Recently, we asked a group of administrators in a large school district to explicate in writing their experiences of the challenges around professional learning and what it would take to move professional learning in their schools and in the district to a more authentic place. Although there was a range of responses, from teacher stress, to lack of understanding, to negative school culture, to difficulty getting authentic teacher "buy in," by far the most common response we got was about lack of time. This is in line with what we've repeatedly heard from both teachers and administrators, as "lack of time" is consistently cited as the number one barrier to implementing authentic professional learning. There is an inherent problem with this explanation, though, that comes by way of an implicit assumption. That assumption is that people are confident that they are already using the time they do have to its greatest potential. But for reasons that you will come to understand as you read this book, that often isn't true. For many, having more time likely wouldn't help their professional learning be more effective at all because doing *more* work still doesn't make it the *right* work. If Greenway's teachers had double the amount of time to spend on their PLC meetings, for example, would the PLC be any more effective? Probably not. The teachers would probably just be doing more work and be more tired and perhaps be more frustrated if they weren't seeing results. We would tell the teachers at Greenway the same thing we tell the administrators and teachers that we work with: Before you try to come up with ways to stretch the clock and make more time, it's important to figure out if the time you already have is being used to its greatest potential—that is, are you doing the *right* work? Our goal in this book is to show what the right work looks like and how to facilitate this kind of true professional learning with others. But before we explain that further, it's important to think about why professional learning is essential in the first place. Why are we even putting such an emphasis on professional learning?

Why Does Professional Learning Matter So Much?

Ask a group of people (in or out of education) what they think is the most significant predictor of student achievement, and you'll likely hear something about socioeconomic status, parental education, geography, or one of many other variables based on a child's family background. While these factors certainly contribute, there has been significant research concluding that regardless of background, the quality of classroom practice that a child encounters has unmatched potential with respect to influencing student learning and achievement. What teachers are doing in classes with students on a daily basis has the greatest potential to influence the academic outcome for students, and the more challenged students are in social capital terms, the more true this is (Darling-Hammond, 2000; Hattie, 2009; Marzano, Pickering, & Pollock, 2001; Nye, Konstantanopooulos, & Hedges, 2004). This makes the goal for teachers seem quite simple: Engage in high-quality classroom practice and your students will succeed. If only it were so simple!

In fact, this awareness is an important first step. It is crucial to understand that high-quality teaching is essential for students to succeed. Many teachers are well aware of the areas in which their students are struggling. Assessment data has helped teachers and administrators determine areas of urgent student learning needs. For example, we often hear administrators saying that their assessment results have indicated that students have difficulty making inferences in reading comprehension or practicing critical thinking. Pinpointing the specific areas where students are struggling is important, but what comes next is even more important, and this is the part that frequently gets left out. It is often assumed that the problem is the identification of what students need to learn, and that once teachers know what students need to learn, they will teach it. But research (e.g., Katz & Earl, 2005) has shown that identification isn't the primary problem; the problem is that teachers often don't know what to do about it. A teacher we know once summed it up succinctly when she said, "I know how to teach fractions; I just don't know what to do when they don't get it!" After identification of student learning needs comes the step where people recognize that if students are struggling with fractions, for example, then teachers need to think about the way in which they teach fractions. Simply knowing what students need to learn is not enough. If student achievement is so strongly dependent on classroom practice, then teachers need to think about how they are teaching in the areas in which students are not achieving as well as they may like.

That said, for the most part, it is likely the case that teachers are already teaching to the best of their abilities (as indicated by the teacher in the anecdote above). Teachers are in the profession because they want to make a difference and contribute to their students' success, and we don't believe that many teachers are holding out and not doing the best they can. We don't, for example, regularly hear teachers say, "These students don't deserve my best lesson on fractions; I'm saving that for students who are more deserving!" This means that you can't simply say to teachers, "It's fractions that your students are struggling with, so teach fractions in a way that makes them understand." We know that teachers are already doing their best.

Simply knowing the areas in which students are struggling is not enough for teachers to be able to teach differently. So what comes next? It is important to understand that teachers teach what they know about a concept. Changing teaching means changing the understanding that underlies the teaching. Sticking with the example of fractions, if teachers are going teach fractions differently (so that students understand fractions differently), then teachers need to learn something new about fractions and about teaching fractions. If they don't learn something new, then they don't have any basis on which to make a change in their classroom practice. The idea is that learning something new (about fractions, in this case) will make teachers understand fractions in a way that makes it impossible for them to continue teaching fractions in the way they were teaching them before. So, learning something new creates the impetus to change the way they're teaching the concept.

This is the foundation of our model (see Figure 1.1). Student achievement is most influenced by classroom practice, and classroom practice is most influenced by teacher learning. Teaching something differently depends on teachers learning something new. It is the *learning* that is key here. In fact, the idea of *learning* in and of itself is even more important than the content area in which the learning is taking place. The requirement to learn new content will always be a part of any professional's job, teachers included. The real power comes in knowing *how* to go about doing that: in having the stance, strategies, and skills to know *how to learn.* Yes, teachers often need to learn something new about the particular content area (fractions in this case) in order to be able to change their practice, but it is knowing *how to learn* that is the transferable skill. In essence, teachers, like all professionals, must learn *how to learn* something new. This will be applied to learning about fractions, as well as every other content area in which the teacher has a learning need. The investment in *learning how to learn* is the one that will yield the greatest return.

Knowing that classroom practice is key to changing student achievement, many have tried to influence classroom practice through professional development (PD). The logic is that if teachers learn something new (through PD activities), they will teach differently and have a positive impact on their students. However, as we will see in Chapter 3, the link between professional development and teacher practice is often weak (for example, see Wallace, 2009). Even in areas that have strong research support, current models of professional development tend to be fairly ineffective in changing teacher practice. Thus, while the logic makes sense, the connection between professional development and changed practice breaks down at some point during implementation. This is a key foundational tenet on which this book rests; that is, that professional development often fails to make a real impact on its participants because it tends not to do enough to respect the psychological definition of learning—a *permanent* change in thinking or behavior. Professional development is often not about learning at all. Learning that changes what people

Figure 1.1   The Path of School Improvement

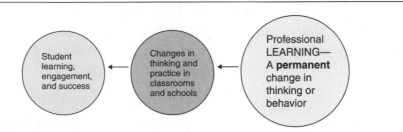

think and how they behave requires conceptual change. Conceptual change happens when people make their current beliefs explicit, subject them to scrutiny from themselves and others, consider how new information either fits or challenges their existing beliefs, and then make permanent changes to what they know and do. It is rarely the case that professional development activities encourage this kind of deep thinking and change, but this is how new learning happens, and (as we've argued above) new learning is required to change classroom practice. From our perspective, this is why the connection between professional development and teacher practice is weak—the actual professional *learning* is often missing. Enabling this sort of true professional learning is what this book is all about.

In an earlier book, *Building and Connecting Learning Communities: The Power of Networks for School Improvement* (Katz, Earl, & Ben Jaafar, 2009), we articulated and unpacked our model for learning communities in depth, focusing on the implications for cross-school networked learning communities in addition to individual school PLCs. Specifically, we explored what our research has identified as the three key enablers of professional learning that are the precursor to changed classroom practice: the practice of establishing and supporting clear and defensible *learning foci* for students, teachers, and leaders; the practice of *collaborative inquiry* that challenges thinking and practice; and the practice of *instructional leadership* (both formal and informal). These are the three enablers of the kind of professional learning that is about permanent change in thinking or behavior, and they will be unpacked further in Chapter 4. Going back to our opening example of Greenway School, it is likely that David's PLC is struggling with all three of these. There is the lack of a clear professional learning focus, difficulty with the practice of collaborative inquiry, and a principal struggling with how to effectively lead learning. And the result is an environment of clutter and activity, and likely of little impact on students.

In this book, we follow the same logic as in the last in terms of the importance of the enablers, but here we emphasize the connection between the enablers and the kind of learning that changes thinking and practice (i.e., how focus, collaborative inquiry, and instructional leadership actually enable real professional learning), as well as the barriers that get in the way of the implementation of these enablers. The logic of the current book (see Figure 1.2) goes like this: to change student achievement, it is necessary to change classroom practice, and changing classroom practice requires new learning. From our perspective, it is these three things—learning foci, collaborative inquiry that challenges thinking and practice, and instructional leadership—that enable such learning. But putting focus, collaborative inquiry, and instructional leadership in place does not happen easily. There are significant barriers to effective implementation. People need to understand what these barriers are and how they prevent learning from happening, and then they need to intentionally *interrupt* them to enable the new learning. Learning is critical, and it's crucial to understand how to facilitate real professional learning and intentionally interrupt the things that get in the way.

Facilitation as Interruption

This book is about facilitating professional learning, and it is important to understand what we mean by *facilitation*. We have already said that the reason true learning is so difficult is because there are many barriers that get in the way of it. When left to their own devices, people's natural propensities are to shut down opportunities for real new learning. Being able to learn in ways that change practice and have a positive impact on students requires purposeful facilitation. We think of this kind of facilitation as *interruption*: an intentional interruption of

Figure 1.2　Building Capacity for Focused Professional Learning

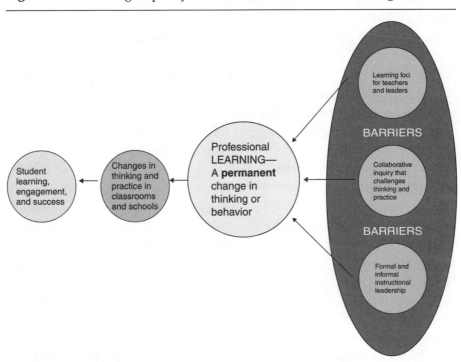

the subtle supports that work to preserve the status quo (the status quo being the *avoidance* of learning). When we talk about facilitation, we are not talking about a dedicated person who has the job (e.g., "the facilitator"). We are arguing that facilitation of learning is a role that *someone* has to intentionally play (and the "someone" can be anyone and can frequently change). The role of facilitation can be undertaken by anyone who has the responsibility of facilitating learning, regardless of who they are and what their formal position is. A facilitator of professional learning may be a formal leader (e.g., district leader, principal, consultant, etc.) or an informal leader (e.g., teacher who takes the responsibility of facilitating the learning of colleagues), and sometimes people even facilitate learning for themselves. The crucial point is that our conception of facilitation entails interrupting the status quo of professional learning in order to enable new learning that takes the form of permanent changes in thinking and practice.

The Sequence of What You'll Learn in This Book

This book is organized into six chapters: In Chapter 2, "The (Very) Hard Work of Learning," we take a step back and examine in depth what learning is from a psychological perspective (a permanent change in thinking or behavior) and why it is so difficult to make it happen. Think about these questions: Have you ever participated in a PD session where you really did think the ideas were meaningful, and you were inspired to change your practice, but then you returned to your school and life got busy and you never really thought about that session again? Do you think you really learned anything from that session? Chapter 2 will take up these questions and others like them. In Chapter 3, "The Problem With Professional Learning," we describe how educators typically try to enable learning—through professional development activities—and why this is problematic from a true learning orientation. As we briefly articulated already, despite the fact that the goal of professional development is to change classroom practice and influence student achievement, most professional development doesn't actually do this because it tends not to be about learning. Have you ever been sitting in a PD session in a big ballroom of a hotel or conference center and wondered how you will actually use what you are hearing about in your day-to-day work as a teacher or administrator? Chapter 3 will explore this question and others like it. In Chapter 4, "How Do Focus, Collaborative Inquiry, and Instructional Leadership Enable Learning?" we look at how professional learning that does have the potential to impact on teacher practice and student achievement happens, specifically examining how it is enabled through focus, collaborative inquiry, and instructional leadership. We specifically articulate how each of these enablers assists in making real professional learning possible, to help give you a clear image of what you might like to see happen.

You will likely finish Chapter 4 thinking, "So why is this so hard? I've learned what learning is and why typical professional development is often not about learning, and I've learned what you need to do to get real learning in place. So what's the holdup? Let's get going and start our learning!" In Chapter 5, "The Barriers: How Our Minds Get in the Way," we describe the holdup. Putting the enablers (focus, collaborative inquiry, and instructional leadership) into place isn't easy or simple because the enablers are embedded in some major psychological barriers that interfere in the professional learning setting. In essence, human beings are predisposed to avoid learning (in the way that we've defined it) as much as possible, and so people unknowingly work very hard to *not learn*. One thing that all of us as human beings tend to do to avoid new learning (i.e., change) is interact with the world in a way that seeks to confirm what we already think, believe, know, and do, rather than challenge it. As an example, have you ever noticed the way you approach reading a professional article? Imagine you're asked to read an article and highlight the points you consider to be important. Most people will highlight points in the article that they agree with or that confirm their existing practices and rarely highlight ideas that challenge them. This small but relatable example illustrates how people (unknowingly) try to maintain the status quo and avoid challenge. Chapter 5 will look at this *confirmation bias* and other psychological biases like it. What all the biases have in common is that they are prevalent in all human beings, and they all work to preserve the status quo and inhibit real new learning. These psychological biases are the barriers to real learning that need to be interrupted. In Chapter 6, "Intentional Interruption," we look carefully at the notion of interrupting the barriers to learning. Specially, we explore strategies and methodologies for intentionally interrupting the barriers described in Chapter 5 to ensure that focus, collaborative inquiry, and instructional leadership unfold in a way that truly enables learning.

Time for Reflection

Take some time to think through the following questions:

- How does your PLC compare to Greenway's, the one described at the beginning of this chapter? What are some similarities and differences?
- From what you've read so far, what are your hypotheses about why Greenway's PLC might not be particularly "impactful"?
- Describe your greatest challenge when it comes to professional learning.
- Who facilitates your professional learning? Do you consider yourself a facilitator of professional learning (either for yourself or for others)?

2

The (Very) Hard Work of Learning

Introduction

Some people will be skeptical of the title of this chapter. Is learning really that hard? Don't we automatically—as human beings—know how to learn? Aren't we learning all the time? A very large body of research would suggest otherwise. We are definitely not "learning all the time." In fact, despite being in the "learning profession," most of us don't understand what learning really is. This chapter provides the psychological perspective on learning and why it is so difficult, with school-based examples to illustrate it.

What Is Learning?

If you search online for definitions of the word *learning*, these are the sorts of things that you will find:

- Acquiring new knowledge, behaviors, skills, values or preferences. ("Learning," n.d., Wikipedia)
- The cognitive process of acquiring skill or knowledge. ("Learning," n.d., WordNet Search)
- The acquisition of knowledge or skill. It occurs in, and may lead to changes in, the brain. (National Institute of Health, n.d.)
- Knowledge acquired by systematic study in any field of scholarly application. ("Learning," n.d., Dictionary.com)

This is only a sampling of definitions. Try looking it up yourself and you will see many definitions, but most include some aspects of what you see above. The first definition is probably most like what you might expect. Poll a group of people and ask them what learning means, and this is the sort of answer you'll likely get: Learning is about acquiring new knowledge, skills, or behaviors (values and preferences may not come to mind as quickly). That seems right, doesn't it? When people learn, they are acquiring something new. The second definition is similar, but it adds in the word *cognitive*: "The cognitive process of acquiring skills or knowledge." Saying that learning is a cognitive process means that it is related to mental activity, like thinking. That sounds okay too. The third definition is similar to the second, but instead of saying "cognitive," it specifically refers to the brain. "Learning occurs in the brain and may lead to changes in the brain." You likely think about the brain as the place where learning happens, but you might not explicitly think about the brain changing. We'll get back to this a bit later. The final definition of learning refers to knowledge acquired through systematic study. This isn't really contrary to any of the other definitions; it simply refers to one specific way in which learning can occur—through study.

From our perspective, none of these definitions is wrong. But we do believe that they are all missing one crucial aspect: a reference to a *permanent* change. If you continue searching definitions of learning, you may also see something that looks like this:

> Psychology—Any relatively permanent change in behaviour that occurs as a direct result of experience. ("Psychology," n.d.)

Many online dictionaries will list a definition similar to this but will mark it with an asterisk to say that it is a *psychological* definition of learning. The way psychologists have defined learning for decades, however, represents what we see as the most promising and valuable definition for directing our efforts at professional learning for (and in) schools. In fact, our definition of choice would probably look like the following one:

> Learning is the process through which experience causes permanent change in knowledge or behavior. (Woolfolk, Winne, & Perry, 2012)

To us (and to most psychologists), learning is defined as a *permanent* change in knowledge or behavior. Actually, if you look closely at the third definition for learning above (the one that refers to the brain), this idea of permanent change is somewhat reflected, though it appears quite subtly. To say that learning occurs in the brain, and may lead to changes in the brain, suggests that there is some permanence to learning. But we would prefer to address this permanence more explicitly, as the definition by Woolfolk et al. (2012) does.

Learning (as a Permanent Change) Is Not Easy or Natural

While most psychologists would probably agree with the definition of learning as a permanent change in knowledge or behavior, if not define it like that themselves, it's likely not the definition we'd find among other groups of practitioners. When we polled a group of teacher candidates on the definition of learning, we got almost no responses that included reference to permanent change. But the inclusion of the word *permanent* in our definition is crucial, and it is one of the foundations on which this book lies. Think of what this means. It means that there are a plethora of things out there that are typically considered to be *learning* that we are asking people to exclude. And this exclusion might be very difficult to accept. This more rigorous definition of learning means that sitting in a workshop may not be learning, reading a book may not be learning, and students may not be learning each and every day when they're in school. It all depends on whether or not these activities contribute to a *permanent* change in knowledge or behavior. One person we worked with told us: "What is learning? Learning is everything! I'm learning every day. I'm a life-long learner!" This sounds nice, and we wish that it were true, but it isn't—at least not for the majority of people. Despite the surrounding rhetoric to the contrary, most people are not learning every day. How often are you really altering your thinking or behavior in a permanent way? It is true that everyday life is filled with *opportunity* for learning. But in reality, and as you will come to understand, people are far more likely to shut down those opportunities than to take advantage of them. Everyone certainly has a lifelong *potential* for learning, but it turns out that most people are more likely to be "lifelong avoiders of learning" than "lifelong realizers of learning."

So, how and why does this happen? Very simply, all human beings, by virtue of our cognitive architecture, have a natural predisposition to preserve and conserve their existing beliefs, understandings, and behaviors. We do not seek out challenge; we seek to preserve the status quo. Do you wake up each morning and say, "Today I really hope that someone will challenge what I think, believe, and know"? Probably not! You most likely wake up in the morning and say something quite to the contrary, something like, "Please let today be smooth with no obstacles or curveballs coming my way." People prefer not to be challenged and don't naturally go out of their way to challenge their current thoughts and beliefs, because challenge creates discomfort. You might find this surprising, but cognitive scientists have been pretty convincing at showing that the human brain is far better programmed for survival than it is for learning (Willingham, 2009). That's why we—as human beings—are more likely to avoid challenge than we are to seek it out. So people go a long way to avoid being challenged. In fact, people regularly commit "thinking errors" (Stanovich, 2009) to trick themselves into preserving the status quo of beliefs, understandings, and practices. (These thinking errors are described in detail in Chapter 5.)

People often talk about the fact that "birds of a feather flock together," and this can be explained in relation to avoidance of challenge, because people who are "like us" are unlikely to challenge us in the ways that bring about discomfort. In fact, while "birds of a feather flock together" and "opposites attract" are both statements that are commonly bandied about, there is only research-based evidence to support one of them—the former. There is actually no evidence that opposites attract (Passer, Smith, Atkinson, Mitchell, & Muir, 2005). People have a natural propensity to surround themselves with others who are similar to them and tell them what they want to hear. In contrast, they put distance between themselves and those who would likely challenge their cognitively comfortable status quo.

Many people believe that they don't fall prey to this preservation and conservation bias. You may be reading through this section and thinking to yourself, "This sounds a lot like other people I know, but I'm different, I don't have a problem with being challenged." But in reality, most people do avoid challenge in this way and try to stick with the comfortable and familiar. Think of the last time you were involved in a professional disagreement. What did you do when your colleague disagreed with you? Did you embrace this difference of opinion and ask her to explain the different perspective? Did you listen to her perspective and eventually integrate her ideas with yours to develop your own new understanding? If you are like most people, then the answer to these questions is probably "no." For example, one of us recently witnessed the following exchange between two teachers: It was a junior division meeting and the activity was moderated marking. Teachers brought in student work examples of opinion paragraphs, and they were looking at topic sentences. In this activity, the teachers were first asked to work in pairs and consider the work that they had each brought to the meeting. One teacher presented her student work sample to the other, expressing her belief that it was a well-written topic sentence. The other teacher, while agreeing that the sentence was well written, felt that it was actually a more appropriate topic sentence for an argumentative paragraph as opposed to an opinion paragraph. The first teacher immediately got defensive, in both verbal and nonverbal ways, and said that according to how she'd taught the lesson, the student had done the appropriate thing. She then declared that it was time to look at the next piece of work. There was no conversation or question about why the other teacher thought differently.

You can probably identify with this example from the perspective of both teachers. Most people have at some point been the ones to make waves and disagree with or challenge someone else's practice, and most have also been the ones to get defensive when someone else disagreed with them. When faced with a potential professional conflict like this, the first inclination that people tend to have is to respond in the way the presenting teacher did in this example—avoid the challenge. Most people don't spend the time trying to understand someone else's perspective, and they work (sometimes very hard) to hold onto their own as tightly as possible. In fact, when confronted with this kind of conflicting information, the first reaction is to avoid it. "He doesn't agree with me? He just doesn't know enough!"

Sometimes, when confronted with something new, avoidance isn't an option. It isn't possible to ignore it or run in the opposite direction. Instead, what people will commonly do is try to transform the novel into the familiar. This notion of *assimilation* was first described by the cognitive psychologist Jean Piaget (1936/1952). In assimilation, people change new information to fit with already existing beliefs, rather than changing the beliefs to fit the information. Take this fairly basic example. When young children first learn about four-legged animals, they often refer to them all as "dogs." Dogs are typically the first four-legged animal that children learn about, and all subsequent four-legged animals may be called dogs too. A young child coming across a horse for the first time, for instance, may call it a "big doggie." This is because the child is trying to fit this new information (a different animal that has some similar features to a dog) into an already existing understanding of four-legged animals (that they are called dogs). Instead of immediately changing the schema (the term used by Piaget to describe the organization of people's knowledge in an area) about animals, she tries to transform the experience to fit with what she already knows and calls the horse a big dog. In other words, she assimilates. This is exactly the phenomenon that one of us experienced en masse when cooperative learning first became an established presence on the educational landscape. Teachers in many, many classrooms started calling all forms of student group work cooperative learning. And they insisted (and completely believed) that they were already "doing" cooperative learning. But most of them weren't. While the small group component was present (because it already had been in the past), other essential criteria such as interdependence, individual and group accountability, intentionally taught interpersonal skills, and group processes were absent. But people were assimilating—trying to make the new idea of cooperative learning fit with what they already knew and were doing, without making any changes.

Learning as Conceptual Change

Let's momentarily return to our "big doggie" example. We have shown that the first inclination, when faced with information that conflicts with current beliefs, is to try to avoid or assimilate. But eventually, the child in our example figures out that this "big doggie" doesn't sit, or bark, or fetch, or do anything else doglike, and she is forced to confront her schema about animals and *change* it to accommodate what she has learned (i.e., that a horse is also a four-legged animal but is different from a dog). This notion of *accommodation* (Piaget, 1936/1952)—changing beliefs and understandings to fit new information—is the kind of learning that embodies conceptual change. When it isn't possible to avoid a new idea, or to turn it into something familiar (assimilation), people are forced to accommodate and revise their cognitive structures to fit the new evidence. Accommodation is conceptual change—changing existing conceptions and restructuring prior knowledge to come to a new understanding that goes beyond what is known already. If you think back to our definition of learning as a permanent change, you will understand why accommodation is the kind of learning that we believe is necessary.

A favorite metaphor of ours that we think does an excellent job of illustrating the effortful (and in fact uncomfortable) process of conceptual change comes by way of a children's toy that has been around—pretty much in its original incarnation—for decades. Take a moment and picture one of those "shape sorter" children's toys that encourage young kids to learn their shapes by sorting. The toy typically involves some kind of container (a ball or a box, for example) with holes of varying shapes, such as a circle, a square, a triangle, a star, a heart, an oval, etc. Inside the container, different plastic shapes are stored, and the objective is to take out all of the shapes and have the child drop them back into the container through the appropriate holes. Now, imagine an approximately one-year-old child coming across this toy for the first time. The parent has dumped all of the shapes out, and the child picks up a yellow circle. He likely puts it in his mouth, decides it's not too tasty, and then tries to figure out what he's meant to do with it if not eat it. He might know that it is yellow (if he's learned his colors) but doesn't know it's called a circle. The committed parent, wanting to ensure success for the child, has now oriented the shape sorter such that the hole that will fit the circle is facing upward, toward the child. The child drops what he doesn't yet know is a circle into the appropriate hole. The circular shape block disappears, and the parents proceed with what we, in psychology, call *positive reinforcement*. They clap, give the child a high five, and maybe even pull out the digital camera to capture this moment of brilliance for all posterity. Now, the effect of positive reinforcement is that it makes behavior more likely to be repeated so the child attempts to repeat what he's just experienced as a success. He picks up the next yellow piece of plastic. We know it to be triangle, but to him, it's the same as the last piece—it looks, feels, and (maybe even tastes) the same. And so he tries to repeat the action. He tries to put it into the round hole. But it doesn't fit!

What happens next? The child's facial expression changes, as smiles are replaced with a look of consternation. The physical "pushback" from the shape sorter creates a state of psychological discomfort—what we call *cognitive dissonance*. A whine or two may even follow. What happens next usually depends on what kind of parents the child has. If they subscribe to the "my job is to help him feel successful" parenting philosophy, they'll likely take the child's hand and guide it away from the round hole and over to the triangular hole. Alternatively, they might be the kind of parents who believe that it's never too early to start learning that the world is full of challenges and that sweating it out builds character, in which case they'll decide not to intervene. The child will likely try with all his might to push that triangle into the round hole, and the uncomfortable feeling will become greater. And eventually (though likely not at that moment or even the next time the child plays with the toy), the child will figure it out and will realize that the triangle piece goes in the triangular hole, rather than the round hole. That is, the child will come to learn that there are different shapes out there and that triangles and circles aren't the same thing. The shape sorter is a tried and true children's toy that has endured over decades because it works; it promotes conceptual change—actually changing existing conceptions of the world, in this case about shape.

This is conceptual change. It involves some sort of pushback—when beliefs or practices are called into question and challenged in ways that require a revision to what we think, believe, know, and do. The child in our example learns to accommodate his understanding of shape—that circles and triangles are different. The pushback or resistance from the shape sorter in response to the attempts to treat the triangle and the circles as the same is a critical—if not *the most* critical—component in the learning process. The experience of cognitive discomfort is not an unfortunate consequence of new learning; it is an essential prerequisite of new learning. If all of the holes on the shape sorter were big enough to allow every piece to fit in regardless of shape, the toy wouldn't work as the intended learning tool for shapes that it is. In the world of young children's experiential learning, the dissonance-creating conditions (the pushback) usually come from the physical environment. In the adult world of professional learning, the challenge isn't usually physical. Rather, it comes by way of other people, whose ideas, beliefs, understandings, and practices are different. But it is no less important as a foundational ingredient of real new learning. And you want to intentionally create the conditions for it to be there.

Suppose you are sitting with a colleague, engaged in a moderated marking activity on a piece of student work—an essay that is supposed to be an example of persuasive writing. You might say to your colleague, "Isn't this great persuasive writing? Doesn't this student really get it?" Your colleague responds with, "Well, I do think this student has done a nice job arguing his opinion, but I'm not sure he's figured out the part about having to convince the reader. I don't see evidence of convincing here. I wonder if the student understands that persuasion isn't only about arguing an opinion but is also about convincing the reader."[1] Immediately, you think about your own understanding of persuasive writing. You're not actually sure if *you've* ever considered the fact that persuasive writing includes this component of needing to convince the reader. Maybe it doesn't, and your colleague is mistaken. But maybe she isn't. You start to get that uncomfortable feeling that most of us get when we are being challenged.

---

[1] This conversation is adapted from Little & Curry (2008).

What do you do next? If you're like most people, the first thing you might try to do is avoid having to deal with this challenge (as we saw in the topic sentences example above). You might say to yourself, "What does she know?" and try to move on as quickly as possible, perhaps by saying, "I really do need to get back to preparing my class for tomorrow now." Alternatively, you may try to assimilate what your colleague is saying into your existing understanding of persuasive writing. You might tell yourself, for instance, that a well-argued opinion is really the same thing as convincing the reader because the latter clearly depends on the former. This would be an attempt to assimilate your colleague's statement into your already existing beliefs, without having to make any change to what you know or do. However, if you really force yourself (or more likely, as you will see throughout this book, if someone else helps you create the conditions to force yourself), you may take the time to really listen to your colleague's perspective, do some additional investigating and thinking, and eventually accommodate by revising your schema for persuasive writing to include (and differentiate) the component of convincing the reader.

This is conceptual change. First, you engage in a process to make your implicit beliefs explicit (in this case, you make your beliefs about persuasive writing explicit). Second, you consider the ways in which your current beliefs may be inadequate (e.g., you consider whether the idea of convincing the reader fits with your belief about persuasive writing and how it may be missing). Finally, you integrate old and new information to form your new beliefs (e.g., you accommodate your existing understanding of persuasive writing to include the new information). This seemingly simple (at least to describe) model of conceptual change describes the kind of learning that we believe is necessary for fundamental school improvement. But it is far from easy to attain. The human brain throws all kinds of obstacles in the way. These obstacles are things that we need to learn to intentionally interrupt, and they will be described in detail in Chapter 5.

It's important to recognize that even when you really are open and do listen, you may not—nor should you—always end up with revised understandings. What matters is that you resist the natural temptation to shut down opportunities for real new learning. When people start to get that dissonance or discomfort, their temptation is often to interpret the feeling as a sign that something is wrong. Instead, they need to learn to embrace the feeling and understand it as a sign that something is right. In other words, that feeling means that learning is coming!

To enable this kind of real learning, professional learning encounters need to take steps to encourage this kind of conceptual change, but as you will see in the next chapter, they often don't. The typical kinds of professional development opportunities don't usually create the conditions for the requisite challenge, and instead, they allow participants to default to avoidance or assimilation. How often, for example, have you sat in a professional development session and thought to yourself, "That [what the presenter is talking about] is what I already do in my class. I just call is something different"? This way of thinking is an attempt to assimilate new information with current beliefs and practices, without making changes. Typical forms of professional development tend not to encourage accommodation or conceptual change. The following chapter describes the "problem" of typical professional learning—specifically, why professional learning in its typical forms often fails to equate to the kind of learning we have described in this chapter.

Time for Reflection

Consider the following questions:

- Did the definition of learning—as a *permanent* change in knowledge/behavior—articulated in this chapter surprise you? Why or why not?
- Using this definition of learning, can you think of a time when you thought you had learned something but you now realize that you may not have?
- How were you feeling as you read this chapter? Were you comfortable with what you were reading, or did it make you uncomfortable in any way? If you are feeling somewhat uncomfortable, why do you think that might be and how might that be a good thing?
- Can you think of an example of a "shape-sorter" type of learning experience from your own life, one where there was pushback on your thinking in a way that felt uncomfortable but ultimately resulted in a new understanding?

3

The Problem
With Professional
Learning

Introduction

This book is about problem solving: solving the problem of professional learning that often isn't about learning. When talking about problem solving, psychologists often refer to the research on expertise. How do experts—in any domain—solve problems, and how does their problem-solving approach differ from that of novices? What research has found is that experts are significantly faster than novices at all stages of problem solving other than one—the problem identification stage (Glaser & Chi, 1988), or what we like to call "problem analysis" (making sure you actually understand what the problem is all about). Experts actually spend significantly more time than novices unpacking a particular problem and mapping out the requirements before jumping into a solution. Once they start working, they do it quite quickly, but they spend significant time up front ensuring that they completely understand the problem before acting. Experts realize that a very important part of any solution is to really understand the problem and that, when you really understand the requirements of a problem, the way forward will likely be met with success.

We need to act like experts when it comes to our problem analysis. We need to spend the time up front really trying to understand the problem at hand. One thing that often differentiates educators from other professionals, such as physicians or lawyers, is that we tend to spend quite a bit less time on this kind of problem analysis and more time on activity. In medicine or law, for example, the success of a professional's actions (e.g., medical treatment or a legal argument) very much depends on the extent to which the individual understands the nature of the problem. In education, we tend to spend much less time on the analysis and a lot more time on the "doing." Look at professional development as an example. People tend to try all sorts of things, often at the same time, without really knowing what "problem" they're trying to respond to. What they often forget is that, just like in other professional domains, the success of the activities also strongly depends on the extent to which people understand their "problems of practice" because we need to make sure the activities being implemented are the right ones. It's crucial to do this within schools and professional learning communities (PLCs), as we'll look at later. But importantly, we also need to do it here, in this book. We need to understand the "problem" that this book is responding to, and this is the problem of professional development—that typical professional development often fails to lead to real professional learning. So before we start talking about solutions, we need to spend the time making sure that we really understand the problem. This chapter devotes itself to this task of problem analysis. We examine what typical professional development looks like and why it often fails to equate to "real learning" for its participants. So let's get started.

There has been significant research examining the relationship between professional development, teacher practice, and student achievement. It has been well established that the link between teacher practice and student achievement is strong (e.g., Marzano, 2003; Sanders & Horn, 1994; Wright, Horn, & Sanders, 1997). In fact, as outlined in Chapter 1, numerous researchers have concluded that the quality of classroom practice is the single biggest predictor of student achievement. If improving teacher practice is the best way to improve student achievement, the subsequent challenge has been framed as one of going to scale: How to get high-quality practice into all classrooms. Professional development has been the vehicle of choice for making an impact on teacher practice that translates to changes in student achievement. However, research has found that the effects of professional development on teacher practice are only small to moderate, with very small (though occasionally significant) indirect effects on student achievement (e.g., Wallace, 2009). In addition, Wallace found that most of the variability in teacher practice in the areas of mathematics and reading is not accounted for by professional development.

What this shows is that the impact of professional development on teacher practice is by no means a given.

Importantly, this is the case in most areas in education, even those that have an extremely strong research base and promise for impact. As a concrete example, let's look at the area of Assessment for Learning, "[the] process of seeking and interpreting evidence for use by learners and their teachers to decide where the learners are in their learning, where they need to go and how best to get there" (Assessment Reform Group, 2002, p. 2). There is a vast amount of research demonstrating the power of Assessment for Learning in impacting on student achievement (e.g., Black & Wiliam, 1998; Crooks, 1988; Popham, 2011). As Popham (2011) recently wrote, "Recent reviews of more than 4,000 research investigations show clearly that when [formative assessment] is well implemented in the classroom, it can essentially double the speed of student learning" (p. 34). Since the Assessment Reform Group in England coined the term *Assessment for Learning* in 1998, it has become ubiquitous in educational systems around the world. It is a well-defined research area with a vast amount of literature. For example, a simple search on "Assessment for Learning" in Amazon brings up almost five thousand title results. And importantly, there has been no shortage of professional development sessions with the goal of building capacity in Assessment for Learning. All that said, however, Assessment for Learning is still absent in most classrooms around the world (Earl, Volante, & Katz, 2011; James & Pedder, 2006). In summary, despite the fact that we know that the practice of Assessment for Learning in the classroom can greatly impact on student achievement and that there are significant professional development opportunities in this area, it is rare to find it in individual classrooms, even rarer to find it in multiple classrooms within a school, and almost impossible to find it at scale within a district.

The purpose of this example is to highlight how difficult it is to get from research to practice through professional development. Current models of professional development, even when working in areas that have a strong research support (such as Assessment for Learning) are fairly ineffective in changing teacher practice. The gap between knowing and doing is huge. Even when there is a robust knowledge base, as there is with Assessment for Learning, it has proven difficult to build teacher capacity in ways that change their classroom practices. Why is this? Why is professional development so often not making a difference for teachers, and ultimately, for students?

The Challenge With Traditional Forms of Professional Development

The goal of professional development is for teachers to hone current skills and knowledge as well as to keep abreast of new knowledge, theories, and methods (Borko & Putnam, 1996). More importantly, the hope is that, by participating in professional development, teachers will go back to their classroom and actually teach differently. Traditional professional development usually takes the form of presentations, workshops, conferences, and training sessions that take place in "ballroom" settings. Much of this traditional professional development is organized as top-down or vertical capacity building. This is problematic in the sense that vertical capacity building can't possibly be "just in time" and "job embedded" in the way that individual schools and teachers often need it to be. Individual schools and teachers are participating in district level professional development that is preplanned and therefore unlikely to be as differentiated or contextually relevant as required.

Many schools that we have worked with have reported that the professional development that they are engaged in at the district level is often not connected to the needs of their school in the moment. A secondary school that we were recently working with described this challenge to us. Teachers in this school were working on improving their use of formative assessment and were focusing in particular on using feedback within the context of formative assessment. At a district professional development day, they were invited to a session on classroom assessment and were excited about the link to their work. But it turned out that the session they attended was emphasizing the differences between formative and summative assessments and when the use of each is appropriate. Because the teachers from this school were quite a bit past that point in terms of their learning about assessment, they didn't find the day particularly worthwhile. Of course, it's always useful to hear an important message again, so the teachers still got something out of the session, but there was an opportunity cost in that these teachers could have used the time spent in this session working on something more urgent for them. This is a case where differentiation within a district would be useful, but in reality, how much can a district do this? It's impossible to give every school what they need when they need it. Vertical capacity building can be a challenge in that it often doesn't meet the urgent and real needs of many of those it is intending to cater to.

An added challenge for traditional "ballroom" professional development involves traveling the often insurmountable gap between the ballroom and the classroom. Although professional development participants are often engaged in meaningful conversation and thinking during such sessions, they are much less likely to actually change their practice based on what they heard or talked about during the session. Activities—not learning—often define the substance of such professional development encounters. The focus is more on "professional development objectives" rather than "professional learning outcomes." As you saw in the previous chapter, true *learning* is about a permanent change in thinking or behavior. Engagement or meaningful conversation in a moment that doesn't translate to changed practice would fail to meet this definition of learning. From our perspective, the focus of professional development needs to be on learning outcomes and how participants will behave differently after the "event." It is of course important to point out that many of these kinds of professional development sessions are not actually happening in large ballrooms and are in fact smaller, more personal sessions, with more opportunity for participant interaction and input. That said, the same principles tend to apply in these contexts, as there ends up being just as much gap between the "small room" and the classroom as there is between the ballroom and the classroom.

The pedagogies of all teaching and learning encounters—including professional development opportunities—reflect core assumptions about how learning is understood to take place. For example, traditional pedagogies of professional development often work from the assumption of the mind as devoid of ideas that need to be transferred from the expert to the learner (Olson & Katz, 2001). This is the idea of "mind as container," where the goal is to fill it with knowledge that it is missing. Using this assumption, "teaching becomes an exercise in telling and learning an exercise in remembering" (Olson & Katz, 2001, p. 246). Judging "competence" in an area refers to how big of a gap there is between what individuals were told and how much they remember. This model of learning tends not to work well because it doesn't take into account what we know about how learning really happens. Specifically, this metaphor of the mind as a container that needs to be filled ignores the well-substantiated idea that true learning (as a permanent change in thinking or behavior) happens when the learner is an active participant in constructing knowledge and is constantly thinking about how new information confirms or challenges previously existing beliefs and ideas.

The Challenge With Alternate
Forms of Professional Development

Because traditional professional development often fails to equate to real learning, many have turned to alternate forms of professional development in an attempt to get away from the ballroom and closer to the classroom. One example is the attempt to use modeling or imitation as a way of helping educators to learn new ways of teaching. A popular way this is taken up is through school "walkthroughs," either within one's own school or by visiting another school. The goal of these walkthrough encounters is for participants to *see* evidence of best practice modeled by their colleagues, rather than to just *hear* about alternative ways of teaching in a traditional ballroom setting. These "new and improved" forms of professional development, however, can be just as problematic as the ballroom. As Olson and Katz (2001) describe, in this model, the assumption is that competence is a skill that can be demonstrated and practiced. The problem with this is that it prioritizes *knowing how* (procedural knowledge) over *knowing that* (declarative knowledge), when in fact, it is necessary to possess the declarative knowledge that underlies every procedure. Put slightly differently, the essence of the problem with walkthroughs is that what is most visibly apparent are activities and tangibles, and participants tend to hang on to these observables without an understanding of the underlying knowledge—the *why* behind the observable.

We have been part of many professional development demonstrations that have sought to model classroom-based "high-yield" strategies only to later find an implementation challenge where the "learned" strategy has been imported into another classroom environment but is no longer high yield. Why would that be? Because what made the strategy high yield was the *yield*—the practice worked because of the understanding that anchored the practice. Classroom practice can't truly change in the areas in which it needs to until the *understanding* that is the foundation of the practice changes. Our own work on high-yield classroom assessment practice, for example, has pointed out that the mere presence of assessment "techniques" in the classroom without the underlying understanding that is rooted in "purpose" negates the power of the practice (Earl & Katz, 2006b). Practice is the visible face of understanding, and changing practices means changing understanding. And if a practice changes without the underlying understanding, there is no reason to expect it to have the desired effect on student achievement. The yield won't be there.

The true intent of something like a walkthrough is for it to function as a tool (or activity) that supports the learning—the "it." The tool, however, is not the "it." The learning is the "it." For example, a teacher who is engaged with her own professional learning agenda around increasing student self-regulation might benefit from visiting a classroom with a teacher who is exemplary at this, but only if time is spent on the front end establishing success criteria for the practice and defining the "look-fors" for the walkthrough so as to understand the knowledge that sets the background for what gets noticed or observed, and then discussed afterward. This rarely happens. The more likely alternative is caricaturized by an example we recently witnessed.

At present, there is (rightfully so in our opinion) a major emphasis in our local districts on early learning and a robust kindergarten experience for children. In some schools, kindergarten teachers who have been identified as exemplary are becoming models for other teachers, regularly inviting observers into their rooms. In one of these observation opportunities that we were recently privy to, a particular kindergarten teacher was sitting on a big, purple, inflatable exercise ball doing a shared reading activity with the students on the carpet, when the observers entered her room. There was no discussion of the exercise ball, and it was not clear whether or not it was related to the class activity. All kinds of other interesting features were on display in the classroom, presumably designed to create a rich early literacy environment, such as a morning message board, "reading around the room" signposts, a high-frequency word-wall, and so on. The following week, we spent some time observing the classrooms of some of the participants from that particular walkthrough. Many of the features observed in the exemplary classroom could now be seen in these classes, but one feature was the most prevalent in terms of replicated practice—many of the teachers now led their carpet lessons while sitting on an inflatable exercise ball. When we asked why, the common response was because they'd seen it modeled in the exemplary demonstration class and had assumed that it was a better way to interact with such young children than sitting on a regular chair. Intrigued, we went back to the host teacher to find out the rationale for the exercise ball. And she explained that she has a bad back and sitting on the ball is more comfortable for her! Though this story seems humorous here, examples like this are happening regularly. Procedural knowledge is taken as an end in and of itself—you just need to see practice to do practice. But the logic of "we show, they do" does not take into account how hard learning really is and can end up being a significant waste of time—what we have called an activity trap (Katz, Earl, & Ben Jaafar, 2009)—for all involved.

The Promise of Professional Learning Communities and Why the Challenge Still Exists

Since traditional forms of professional development have been the subject of significant criticism, many school districts have begun to adopt the idea of within- and across-school learning communities as an alternative vehicle for professional development. There have been a myriad of books, including our own, that have described PLCs either within or across schools (e.g., Gregory & Kuzmich, 2007; Hord & Sommers, 2008; Kaagan & Headley, 2010; Katz et al., 2009; Muijs, West, & Ainscow, 2010; Roberts & Pruitt, 2009). The idea behind many of these collaborative models is that "together is better," and the hope is that, if people work together, practice will improve, and student learning and achievement will follow.

Recently, some governments and school districts have been getting behind the idea of cross-school networked learning communities. Networked learning communities (see Katz et al., 2009) work from the premise that job-embedded professional development that is contextually relevant is what really makes a difference for schools and that resources aren't available to do this in a vertical way. The idea of networks involves a shift from a vertical capacity-building notion to a lateral one, where schools in a shared context with similar needs work together. The idea is to create opportunities for educators across different schools to learn *from* one another (when one individual has knowledge that he or she shares with others who need it), to learn *with* one another (when no one in the network has the knowledge, but members collectively pursue it because the need is shared), and to learn *on behalf of* one another (when participants are taking on a collective responsibility for all students in the network schools) (Jackson & Temperley, 2006). Networked learning communities rely on—and work to build—strong within-school PLCs because research (Katz & Earl, 2010; Katz et al., 2009) shows that it is through individual schools that networks are intended to have an effect (on classroom practice and student achievement).

Unfortunately, the rhetoric around PLCs has far outpaced the research (Supovitz, 2006). Although many schools and districts have adopted the language of "professional learning communities," the link between "working together," "changed practice," and "improved student achievement" has been far from clear in implementation. Many seem to believe that simply working "together"—whatever that entails—will lead to positive outcomes, but the research on the efficacy of PLCs is much thinner than we'd hope it to be. In reality, PLCs can fall prey to the same criticisms as traditional professional development. In some cases, PLCs are synonymous with PLC *meetings*, and these simply become "mini-ballrooms." The PLC becomes the venue to "deliver information" or "fill the container" in the same way as typically happens in the ballroom; it's just a smaller ballroom. Again, with little focus on learning outcomes and changed practice, true "learning" remains elusive. PLCs (both within-school and cross-school) can also fall prey to the observation and imitation challenge described above, where a modeling situation is established without the appropriate underlying understanding. For the most part, PLCs are more about *doing* things together, rather than *learning* things together (Supovitz, 2006). Despite the *L* in PLC, there often ends up being a focus on activity rather than learning. In fact, we have often said that some PLCs quickly turn into PACs— professional activity communities. David, the principal of Greenway (the school we described at the beginning of the book), would likely identify with this.

For many schools, the term *professional learning community* means a dedicated meeting that takes place once every other week (or something like that) for an hour or two. We often hear things like "we have our PLC on Thursday at 12:30." But from our perspective, having a strong PLC in a school is much more than a series of "events" (e.g., in-services, book studies, etc.). A strong PLC in a school revolves around learning being central in all interactions and conversations. A two-minute exchange between two teachers, for example, can sometimes be more powerful than a two-hour formal meeting. Let's say, for example, that a teacher runs into the staffroom one day at lunch and says to a colleague, "You won't believe what this student just did. Look at this paper." The colleague (hopefully) isn't going to respond with, "Well, our PLC meeting is next Thursday. You'll tell me about it then." If the colleague starts to ask why that piece of student work is so interesting, why it's different from what the teacher expected, and so on, the encounter can turn into a real learning opportunity for both individuals involved, where beliefs about teaching and learning are possibly challenged and changed. As we pointed out in Chapter 1, people often say that the biggest barrier to professional learning is a lack of time. But it doesn't take more time to have that two-minute conversation in the staffroom. It takes a culture—a learning-driven school in which professionals are constantly asking one another the kinds of questions that challenge existing beliefs and practices and lead to new learning. That's what a true professional learning community is all about.

The Distinction Between Professional Development and Professional Learning

This chapter has described professional development and the challenges that are associated with it leading to real learning for its participants. We have intentionally used the term *professional development* rather than *professional learning* throughout this chapter, although for many, these two terms are used interchangeably. Why is this? Is it because people assume that professional development and professional learning mean the same thing? *Do* they mean the same thing? Many experts have explicitly argued that they don't. As Timperley (2011) writes,

> [T]he term "professional development" has taken on connotations of delivery of some kind of information to teachers in order to influence their practice whereas "professional learning" implies an internal process in which individuals create professional knowledge through interaction with this information in a way that challenges previous assumptions and creates new meanings. (pp. 4–5)

We hope that it is clear by now that we would agree with the distinction made by Timperley, as well as many other experts in the field (e.g., Guskey, 2000). In our view, the two terms are distinct. There is a big leap from *development* to *learning*, and in reality, professional development often doesn't produce learning at all. The term *professional development* describes activities or doings (e.g., you go to an event and participate in activities), but it doesn't describe the extent to which you've changed your beliefs, and it certainly doesn't refer to changed practice. Many professionals describe professional development as something that *happens* to them (e.g., "I got PD on X"), but it can only become learning when we construct new knowledge, and for many of us, this never happens.

We will continue to use both terms (*professional development* and *professional learning*) throughout the book, with the assumption that they are different and that development does not always mean learning. Regardless of your choice of terminology, what matters is that the focus is on learning and improved practice. Remember our definition of real learning—a permanent change in thinking or behavior. Professional development is not professional learning unless it changes the way you think and behave. From our perspective, real professional learning is the product of "shape-sorter" opportunities (remember the analogy from the last chapter?)—opportunities that create dissonance or discomfort for us to work through. People need help in creating these shape-sorter opportunities and in learning to be one another's shape sorters (i.e., create pushback and challenge for one another), and this is what we mean when we say that real professional learning needs to be facilitated. As we've said repeatedly, real learning is not a natural inclination; humans actually evolved to avoid challenge (Willingham, 2009). But if challenge is essential to real new learning, because we don't just want to survive, we want to improve, then we're going to need help. And that's why it's so crucial that professional learning is intentionally facilitated. As we've already said, that facilitator need not be an external facilitator, though it might be. The facilitator can be any individual who is taking responsibility to *intentionally interrupt* the status quo and create shape-sorter opportunities for themselves and others.

Putting Things Together So Far

Taken together, this chapter and the last should give you a good sense of how and why professional development is very different from professional learning. As others (e.g., Hattie, 2009; Levin, 2011) have said, it's not that educators are deprived of knowledge as to what works. Supply isn't the problem. We have a substantial supply of things that we know work or have the potential to work. Interestingly though, most of the work being done in relation to professional development is about coming up with new programs, workshops, and initiatives— essentially adding more items to the menu on the supply side. And teachers and leaders are constantly being offered more and more things to choose from, with a focus on all the different choices. But the problem isn't about supply; it's much more about demand (Elmore, 1996). The teachers and principals who are being asked to choose from the supply menu are rarely asked to think about what they need to learn to support the work that they do with students. There isn't enough of a focus on the demand. The problem really isn't about knowing what works; we know a lot about what works. It's much more about creating opportunities to need and want to *know* (i.e., demand), such that interactions with the supply menu can be purposeful and deliberate.

Now that we have explored what real professional learning is, and how much of what we think about as professional learning might actually not be learning at all, we turn to a consideration of how to purposefully create the conditions for making it happen. This demands a dual strategy of "enabling" and "interrupting," with intentional facilitation as a core dimension of both. In Chapter 4, we provide an in-depth description of what research has identified as the key enablers of professional learning: learning foci for teachers and leaders, collaborative inquiry that challenges thinking and practice, and formal and informal instructional leadership. In Chapter 5, we look closely at the psychological barriers that must be interrupted in order for the enablers to realize their professional learning potential, and in Chapter 6, we describe what interruption of those barriers to professional learning looks like.

Time for Reflection

Take some time to consider the following questions:

- Earlier in this chapter, we said the following: "Professional development is not professional learning unless it changes the way you think and behave." Using this distinction between professional development and professional learning, what were the last three "professional development" experiences that you were part of? Thinking about them now, would you consider them to be professional learning? Why or why not?
- Have you had any professional learning experiences recently that were outside of formal professional development opportunities? What were they, and why would you consider them to be professional learning?

4

How Do Focus, Collaborative Inquiry, and Instructional Leadership Enable Learning?

Introduction

As we mentioned in Chapter 1 (when we explained our model), professional learning is enabled by learning foci for teachers and leaders, collaborative inquiry that challenges thinking and practice, and formal and informal instructional leadership. In this chapter, we look at *how* focus, collaborative inquiry, and instructional leadership enable professional learning. Specifically, what do focus, collaborative inquiry, and instructional leadership look like when they are working to enable true professional learning that changes teacher practice?

A Learning Focus

We often hear people talking about school improvement that's "a mile wide and an inch deep." This kind of school improvement agenda often has little impact because it isn't "focused" enough. Establishing a learning focus means identifying an urgent student learning need (based on evidence) and recognizing that this student learning need indicates a *teacher* learning need. Remember, the link between teacher practice and student learning is a strong and robust one (e.g., Darling-Hammond, 2000; Hattie, 2009; Marzano, Pickering, & Pollock, 2001). If students aren't learning, it raises questions about the efficacy of the teaching practices and, subsequently, the learning needs of the professionals involved. A teacher learning focus emerges from an investigation of what teachers need to learn to support what students need to learn. Teachers may need to learn something content based, or they may need to learn a new instructional or pedagogical strategy to support a particular content piece (we will look at an example in a moment). It is also important to understand that the idea of a learning focus doesn't end with teachers, because the same way that a student learning need defines a teacher learning need, a teacher learning need defines a leader learning need. Determining a leader learning need requires that we ask what leaders need to learn to support what teachers need to learn to support what students need to learn. Put slightly differently, everyone has "a class" (Timperley, 2011). Teachers have students in their classes. Leaders have teachers in their classes. Everyone has to figure out how to best teach their class—whole group, small group, differentiated, one-on-one, etc. A learning focus for leaders could be a content focus or a process focus, like change management. Let's look at an example of the way in which a student learning need defines a teacher learning need and a teacher learning need defines a leader learning need.

Many of the elementary schools that we are currently working with are identifying *inferring* as an urgent student learning need within the literacy domain. Schools are finding that their data—both from large-scale testing and from individual teacher classroom assessments—are pointing to a student learning need around being able to make inferences from text as key reading comprehension skill. One particular school that we recently worked with struggled with turning this identification of the student learning need into a teacher learning focus. At the beginning of the school year, a group of staff (administrators and leaders) sat down over a number of meetings to look at the school's results from the large-scale assessment at the end of the last school year, as well as the previous year's report card data. Through these meetings, the group pulled out inferring as the greatest student learning need. During one particular meeting that we attended, the principal turned to the group and said, "So we've figured out where students are really struggling. But what are we going to *do* about it?" After a long, silent moment, the principal—to break the ice—said, "Maybe we should send a note home to parents telling them to send us a new child next week that knows how to make inferences!" The joke was not lost on the group. It was clear that they understood that this wasn't a problem with the students; it was a problem of teacher practice. One of the teachers then said, "It's hard, because it's not like we're not teaching inferring. It's one of those things that's really hard for students to understand, but I know I can't blame them for not getting it. I look at this data and see that my class isn't an exception. Clearly, what I'm currently doing when it comes to teaching inferring isn't working. But I don't know what else I could do." The principal then replied by saying, "Then maybe as a group of professionals we need to learn something new about teaching inferring. Maybe we need to focus our own professional learning on that."

This moment was really a turning point for the group. They understood that if students were going to understand inferring differently (i.e., better), then it would be because teachers were teaching inferring differently (i.e., better). And they realized that this could only happen if teachers learned something new about inferring—something new about what inferring is, how it is learned, and how to teach it. This is what we mean by a professional learning focus. What do teachers need to learn to support what students need to learn? The goal, then, is for teachers to engage in deep professional learning in a fairly narrow area such that classroom practice will change and student learning will improve. And creating the conditions for this kind of focused professional learning defines a key leadership dimension.

As we said earlier, teacher learning needs define leader learning needs. With respect to the "inferring" problem of professional practice, what do leaders need to learn to support what teachers need to learn to support what students need to learn? Although school leaders likely don't need to learn as much about inferring as teachers (because they aren't the ones actually teaching the students), they do need to learn enough about it to be able to speak a common language and to know what the success criteria look like so that they can help monitor implementation. But beyond content, new learning for leaders often has a change management focus, in which leaders learn how to create the conditions in their schools for teachers to learn about inferring. They may, for example, need to learn how to build a school culture that is learning driven (where teachers are keen to participate in all aspects of a needs-based professional learning process), they may need to learn what it means to establish effective professional learning communities (PLCs) in the school (as a place where real professional learning can take place), or they may need to learn how to work with resistant teachers and get them "on board." The leader learning focus will be driven by the teacher learning focus.

We are often asked how long to stay with a focus. After all, the concept of a focus suggests that, while something is in the foreground as a priority, other things must fade into the background, and some of those are important too. For us, the answer is fairly straightforward—focus is about priority setting, and you stay with a focus until there is evidence to suggest that it is no longer the most urgent student learning need. A focus doesn't change with the seasons, or with the calendar, or on a whim—even if it is a well-intentioned whim. A focus is identified by evidence of student learning need, and changing it will be defined by evidence of practice having made an impact on that student learning need. A focus is not a focus "for life," but it is a focus as long as that continues to be the most urgent need for students (Katz, Dack, & Earl, 2009).

A number of school districts that we work with use six-week collaborative inquiry cycles to guide teacher learning. The idea is to start with a demonstrable area of student learning need (a focus), engage students in a preassessment, review curriculum expectations in relation to the area, moderate the preassessment, examine current teaching practices, work to deepen understanding in the area through new collaborative professional learning, define and implement a new teaching practice, engage students in a culminating assessment, and monitor and evaluate their progress. As you will see when we describe collaborative inquiry that challenges thinking and practice in the next section, we support the use of these kinds of cycles to guide teacher learning as long as the "area" of defined student need is supported by evidence to suggest it is an urgent one. Under those conditions, these kinds of inquiry cycles can be a potentially useful methodology for moving the learning forward. What becomes problematic, however, is when we see administrators (and other practitioners) falling into the "activity trap" (Katz, Earl, & Ben Jaafar, 2009) of sitting down at the June staff meeting to figure out all the cycles for the next academic year. What happens when, at the end of the first cycle, it turns out the intended impact on student learning isn't there? It wouldn't make sense to move on to something entirely new, even if that's what had been planned the previous June. If the cycle is about teacher learning, and teacher learning needs are informed by student learning needs, then the logic would say that if the student learning needs are still there, the teacher learning needs are still there.

A learning focus, by definition, is narrow. It needs to be narrow enough so as to allow teachers to engage in a professional learning process that works to enhance depth of understanding. Breadth and depth are a trade off. A mile wide means an inch deep, and we know that that doesn't work when it comes to changing practice. But a mile deep means an inch wide. And that means we have to be sure that we've got the right inch!

When we first started to work with the notion of focus in various schools and districts, an important and problematic unintended consequence emerged that we subsequently identified and unpacked in our research (Katz & Dack, 2009). Practitioners engaged with the concept of focus through the dominant culture of activity, rather than an alternative culture of learning. What this meant was that focus was interpreted as a teaching focus, not a learning focus. Teachers constantly asked us how they could possibly prioritize something as narrow as "inferring in reading for meaning" in their teaching, given the breadth of the required formal curriculum. A critical distinction was missing. A focus on inferring means that teachers are committed to privileging their own professional *learning* about inferring. However, they are still *teaching* the entire curriculum. Identifying a focus doesn't mean that you don't care about other things. It's simply about moving an urgent (professional) learning need to the foreground.

Focus, as the first of the three key enablers of professional learning, is the *what* of professional learning. It defines what people are committed to learning about in some depth that is needs based. Next, we turn to a consideration of collaborative inquiry that challenges thinking and practice, which we see as the *how* of professional learning. Finally, we will look at instructional leadership, which you can think of in terms of *who* facilitates the learning.

Collaborative Inquiry That Challenges Thinking and Practice

Collaborative inquiry that challenges thinking and practice is the *how* of professional learning (Katz et al., 2009; Nelson, Slavit, Perkins, & Hathorn, 2008). It's the methodology for moving a learning focus forward. Collaborative inquiry includes two components—collaboration (working together) and inquiry (a search for deep understanding). Neither of these are simple concepts. Collaborative inquiry that challenges thinking and practice involves people working together in meaningful ways to deepen understanding and challenge what they already know and do in an area of determined need—what we are calling the focus. A key component of collaborative inquiry is the element of challenge. And so, by definition, collaborative inquiry that works enables real professional learning because it promotes the kind of accommodation and conceptual change that we described in Chapter 2, that is, reconstructing what people think, believe, know, and do.

---

1. Develop an inquiry question: What's your problem of practice and why?

2. Develop a working hypothesis and plan to investigate it: How do you intend to intervene and why?

3. Determine success criteria *and* associated evidence to be collected (and how).

4. Implement the plan.

5. Analyze the evidence in relation to the success criteria.

6. Reflect on the learning.

7. Determine "next practice" for the inquiry cycle to continue.

Collaborative inquiry involves the discipline of working through a framework (Hakkarainen, Palonen, Paavola, & Lehtinen, 2004), like the one explicated in the numbered list. The process begins by collectively developing an inquiry question, which, in essence, involves framing your learning focus as a question or a problem of practice. As we will see in Chapter 6, the fact than it takes the form of a question is important, because human beings tend to be more motivated to answer questions than to simply think about issues. You also want to ensure that your problem of practice is supported by evidence—in other words, that it really is a professional learning need. Next, you develop a working hypothesis and a plan for investigating the hypothesis (what you think might make a difference and how you plan to go about giving it a try). In the third step, you determine success criteria and the associated evidence (how you will know if you've been successful). You then implement your plan and analyze the evidence that you decided was important to pay attention to. Finally, you complete the cycle by reflecting on the process—what did you learn—and determining your *next practice*—where will you go next.

Several of the school districts that we work with use inquiry cycles like this to guide the work that they do in their PLCs. In one particular secondary school, the math department engaged in inquiry-based professional learning because they suspected that they had an issue of professional practice in relation to the construction of their final exams in mathematics. They began by looking for evidence that would confirm or challenge their perceived problem of practice, and they identified a few sources of evidence that did in fact confirm their beliefs—that the problem was really a problem. First, they observed a disconnect between students' grades on their final math exams and their other term marks in the respective classes. Second, they found little consistency between the final math exams in like courses. And third, in examining the contents of the math exams, they found that the questions on the exams were not focusing on enduring curriculum expectations. Taken together, all of this evidence pointed to a problem of practice in relation to the final exams. The department's inquiry question became, how can we improve the construction of our final exams in math? Note that all of this work was about problem identification—about understanding the nature of the professional challenge of practice. It was the first step in the inquiry process, and you can see how involved it was. That's why focus matters. They couldn't do this kind of work for everything. They needed to make sure they had the "right inch"!

Next, the PLC developed their working hypothesis. The hypothesis was that if a set of requirements and supports were intentionally put in place as scaffolds, teachers would understand their assessment and evaluation work differently, and the quality of their final exams would improve. The intervention plan included a few different aspects: First, they decided to invite the district classroom assessment consultant to work with the staff on the purposes of classroom assessment, the difference between various kinds of assessments, and the relationship between assessment, evaluation, and reporting. The explicit intention behind this was to learn what makes an exam a high-quality one and how to improve consistency between exams and other in-class assessments. Second, they provided dedicated time for members of the math department to work together to collaborate on building final exams. The purpose of this was to improve the consistency of exams in like classes and stimulate conversations about classroom assessment between teachers who were in different places in their understanding, such that those who were more expert could share their wisdom. And third, the school principal put a policy into place that required final exams to be developed and submitted by the end of the first month of the course in which they would ultimately be used. The underlying concern was that students were being "surprised" by things that appeared on the final exam. The rationale behind the policy strategy was that it would require teachers to define the expected learning outcomes for the course early on, such that they could be communicated to the students near the beginning of the course and monitored for understanding along the way.

The group's criteria for success included the presence of more teacher collaboration on exam creation, consistency of exams among like courses, alignment in student grades between final exams and other classroom assessments, and exam questions that focused on enduring curriculum outcomes. Their plan to gather the evidence involved reviewing—in small groups—the exams they developed, keeping track of the frequency of their collaborative efforts on exam construction, comparing term marks to final exam marks in the school's electronic reporting database, and mapping the exams against the learning expectations defined in the curriculum. This was all articulated in the planning stage, prior to the actual implementation.

The PLC then put their plan into action, implementing it over a number of months. They invited the district assessment consultant in; devoted their department meetings to the purposeful activity of collaborating on, and reviewing, their final exams; and instituted the new policy of having the exams ready near the beginning of the semester. They collected the evidence described in the previous paragraph (some throughout the semester and some at the end of the semester once final exams had been graded) and analyzed it in relation to their predetermined success criteria. They found that there was more teacher collaboration within like courses and that the exams were much more consistent across like courses. They also found that, for the most part, students did better on the final math exams than was previously the case. However, there still appeared to be a significant disconnect between grades on final exams and grades on other assessments throughout the term. Although this disconnect was somewhat reduced from previous semesters, it was still quite a bit higher than the school had hoped. In their first PLC meeting after analyzing all the data, they reflected on the process and on what they had learned and began to discuss how they could refine their next inquiry question in relation to the disconnect between exam grades and grades on other assessments in the same course. And the inquiry cycle continued . . .

This detailed example illustrates both the complexity of the inquiry cycle and its power in refining a process and investigating a problem of practice in a systematic way. It also illustrates the importance of each element in the process, right from the very beginning.

Suppose, for example, that this group had assumed that their problem of practice relating to student achievement in math was actually not about issues of disconnect in their exams but rather about something completely different. And suppose further that the group didn't explicitly consider whether or not there was actually any evidence for this alternative problem of practice. The consequence would have been an "expensive" one—a lot of work, but not the right work. In the context of our example, this wasn't as far-fetched as we're making it sound. It almost happened.

When we first came to know this particular school, they already had an established goal of raising student achievement in math, and it was reflected, as with many schools, in their school improvement plan. They had not, however, ever worked with the inquiry process, although they were quite keen when they first heard about it. They were attracted to the authenticity of the process. It relied heavily on professional judgment, and it respected—even relied on—the realities of *their* classrooms and school. Their first efforts at identifying a problem of practice in relation to student achievement in math quickly honed in on poor attendance in math classes. Teachers were of the impression, and had been for years, that low attendance rates were responsible for the achievement challenge. As one teacher put it, "students have to be there to be able to learn!" It was from this that the group derived an early inquiry question: How can we increase attendance in our math classes?

One of us was at the PLC meeting where the group presented their problem of practice around attendance. The original intent was to then spend the meeting constructing a strategy (or several strategies) for dealing with the attendance problem. That didn't happen because the one of us who was there—as an invited critical friend—interrupted (intentionally) and asked what the group was taking as evidence for the problem of practice; that is, how did they know that attendance was *the* problem? Two teachers volunteered to gather some data around student attendance, which really didn't require much more than printing out some attendance reports by course from the school's database, and bring it to the next PLC meeting. At that next meeting, these two teachers presented the data, which turned out to be quite surprising to most in the group. Although the group was correct that attendance was problematic in many math classes (the attendance numbers were in fact lower than in other departments in the school), there was no evidence that attendance was actually linked to poor achievement in math. Specifically, most of the students with the worst attendance rates had average exam grades, while those with the lowest exam marks had missed fewer than five classes over the entire semester. Those students who were struggling on the exams the most weren't absent a lot; they just weren't learning, at least not as measured by the final exam. It was this process that led the group to start looking at the final exams with a more critical eye and to ultimately define the inquiry question that they did (around construction of final exams). Remember, inquiry is about professional learning; in this case, the learning started as soon as we asked the "how do you know" question.

The example illustrates, with some depth, what inquiry can look like when it works, but we haven't yet said much about the collaborative part—*how* educators work together to create the conditions for the inquiry process to truly be a learning one. We mentioned, for instance, that teachers in our example collaborated on the development of final exams for like courses, but what does high-leverage (in terms of promoting real new learning) collaboration look like?

Judith Warren Little (1990) offers a useful four-fold taxonomy for examining collaboration: storytelling and scanning for ideas; aid and assistance; sharing; and joint work. *Storytelling and scanning for ideas* is quick, informal exchanges between individuals that typically happen at a distance from the classroom. In *aid and assistance*, mutual aid or help is readily available when it's asked for, but colleagues are unlikely to offer one another assistance in an unsolicited way. In *sharing*, colleagues make aspects of their work available to others, but there is no commentary on the work and no dimension of challenge. It is in *joint work* where colleagues share responsibility and really believe that they need each others' contributions to succeed. In joint work, ideas are put on the table for discussion, analysis, debate, and challenge. People practicing joint work are challenging one another's assumptions about teaching and learning, are providing feedback to one another (and are also receptive to receiving it from others), and are talking openly about differing views and opinions. This is why we talk about collaborative inquiry *that challenges* thinking and practice. Remember, learning is a permanent change in thinking or behavior. Collaboration that takes the form of joint work is the stuff of shape sorters! It is where people are forced to consider how other people's ideas, or outside evidence, either confirm or challenge what they think, believe, know, and do in an explicit way. We will talk a lot in the next two chapters about why this is so difficult and how we might intentionally interrupt the barriers that get in the way to make it more likely to happen.

Formal and Informal Instructional Leadership

The kind of leadership that enables true professional learning is instructional leadership—leadership related to curriculum, teaching, and learning. When it comes to enabling professional learning, both formal leaders (those who are leaders by virtue of role and position) and informal leaders (those who are leaders by virtue of expertise rather than role or position) play a role. We and others have articulated the distinction between formal and informal leaders elsewhere (for example, see Katz, Earl, & Ben Jaafar, 2009; Spillane, 2006; Timperley, 2011), and it is not our intention to recapitulate the details of that distinction here. This isn't a book about leadership per se. Rather, our goal in this section is to think about leadership in terms of what it means to lead learning. If focus is the *what* of professional learning and collaborative inquiry is the *how*, then instructional leadership is the *who*. But it is not *who learns* (that's everyone's responsibility); it is rather *who leads* the learning. If you are reading this book, chances are that you are, or have the potential to be, a lead learner.

Robinson, Höhepa, and Lloyd (2009) conducted a comprehensive research review on the impacts of leadership on student achievement, with the goal of identifying a set of evidence-based leadership practices that ratchet up the quality of classroom and school practice and that ultimately lead to student achievement. They identified the most impactful leadership dimensions and quantified them by effect size. Five leadership dimensions emerged as especially powerful and significant:

1. Establishing goals and expectations (effect size = 0.42): Includes the setting, communicating, and monitoring of learning goals, standards, and expectations and the involvement of staff and others in the process so that there is clarity and consensus about goals.

2. Strategic resourcing (effect size = 0.31): Involves aligning resource selection and allocation to priority teaching goals.

3. Planning, coordinating, and evaluating teaching and the curriculum (effect size = 0.42): Direct involvement in teaching through regular classroom visits and the provision of feedback to teachers. Direct oversight of curriculum through schoolwide coordination across classes and grades and alignment to school goals.

4. Ensuring an orderly and supportive environment (effect size = 0.27): Protecting time for teaching and learning by reducing

external pressures and interruptions and establishing an orderly and supportive environment both inside and outside classrooms.

5. Promoting and participating in teacher learning and development (effect size = 0.84): Leadership that not only promotes but directly participates with teachers in formal and informal professional learning.

All five dimensions are powerful (in effect size terms), but one cannot help but notice how the last one—promoting and participating in teacher learning and development—stands far above the others. While it's not always the hottest fire that commands a leader's attention, nothing that a leader does has a bigger payoff in terms of enhanced practice and improved student achievement than learning visibly and publicly alongside staff in a school. Our own research (see Katz, Earl, & Ben Jaafar, 2009) has highlighted the important shift of stance away from "lead knower" and toward "lead learner"—from "I lead because I know more" to "I lead because I know how to learn." And in the largest study of its kind on the impacts of leadership in schools, Louis, Leithwood, Wahlstrom, and Anderson (2010) found that high-performing schools benefit from leadership that encourages "professional community," an environment in which teachers collaborate to improve practice, and that broadens the base of leadership to include more than just the principal.

In an earlier book (Katz, Earl, & Ben Jaafar, 2009), we described the *imposter syndrome*, the little voice that we all carry around that says, "I have no idea how I got to be where I am, but I just hope that nobody finds me out!" The imposter syndrome finds its power by making you believe that you are the only one who feels that way (even though you're not), and this is an impediment to real new learning. Real new learning opportunities—the shape-sorter kinds of things—require that we make ourselves vulnerable and that we are explicit about what we don't know and need to understand. The imposter syndrome, by definition, inhibits that. This is why visible and public colearning on the part of administrators is such an impactful dimension of high-leverage leadership. Think about how powerful it is for teachers to hear their principal explicitly question his or her own understanding (or lack thereof) in a public way, in effect giving others on staff permission to "not know" and to learn.

We recently observed the conception of lead learner in action at a PLC meeting in a small elementary school. The school has a focus on balanced literacy, and at this particular meeting, the group was talking about effective Guided Reading strategies. At one point, the school's literacy coach put out a question about teacher practice in relation to Guided Reading, and the conversation ground to halt; no one seemed to want to answer the question. After a long, uncomfortable silence, the principal, who had been a quiet participant in the meeting up until then, spoke up, saying something along the following lines:

> I need to say something before this meeting continues. Our district has had a literacy focus for the past ten years, and I've been a principal in this district for five of them. Before that, I worked on implementing a good balanced literacy program in my own classroom. The term *balanced literacy* has become such a regular part of our lexicon, and we have talked about Guided Reading as a strategy for years. I've asked you, as teachers in this school, many times, to implement a quality balanced literacy program and to protect your time for Guided Reading, and the truth is . . . I don't really know what Guided Reading actually is. I'm supposed to—in fact expected to—be able to walk into each one of your classrooms and know what it looks like. In reality, I don't really know much about it beyond the fact that it involves small groups of kids sitting and reading with a teacher at those purple, half-moon tables that we ordered for all of you last summer . . . I'd be lying to you if I said that this is a comfortable admission. It isn't. It makes we wonder what I'm doing sitting in this seat. But I feel that I have to say that I need to understand Guided Reading better so that I can support you in understanding it better.

You could honestly feel the tension leave the room, and the sighs of relief around the table were audible. The principal had assumed the posture of lead learner. By leading through example, with authenticity and vulnerability, she had made it okay for others to explicitly "not know."

Sometimes, taking the stance of lead learner is less involved, though no less powerful. It's about listening and showing that you are able to relate. In other words, it breaks down the imposter syndrome by saying "me too." A secondary school principal in one of the leader learning networks that we work with told us about an occasion in which he was talking to teachers in his school about their upcoming performance appraisals. Performance appraisals in that district involve a classroom observation by the principal, bookended with a set of conversations with the teacher (pre- and post-observation) to define and debrief the teacher's professional growth goals. Reading the nonverbal cues around room at the staff meeting as he discussed the upcoming performance appraisals, this principal described an atmosphere of trepidation—what we would explain as fear of exposure and evaluation, courtesy of our friend, the imposter syndrome. He proceeded by telling them that he could relate to how they must be feeling. He explained that, when he went through his last principal performance appraisal with his supervisory officer (district administrator) a few months earlier, he was nervous and felt tempted to define a goal for his growth plan that he knew he could meet, just to make himself look good. He told the staff that he had to actively resist this temptation: that he forced himself to remember that the purpose of the growth plan was to identify places where you need to grow and learn. And he described the tension he felt between being authentic and—in his words—"covering his ass." As a lead learner, this principal led by his own example. He gave teachers permission to open themselves up to shape-sorter encounters; to opportunities that likely wouldn't be comfortable but that would be authentic, needs based, and learning driven.

We mentioned at the beginning of this section that, if focus is the *what* of professional learning and collaborative inquiry is the *how*, then instructional leadership is the *who*. But we also said that instructional leadership is not the *who* in entirety, because it's not just leaders who need to learn; the responsibility to learn belongs to everyone. Good instructional leaders *enable* learning—for themselves and for others. And we hope that, if you're reading this book, you see yourself having the potential to be a lead learner in your professional context, whether it's through a formal or informal leadership position.

So, What's the Problem?

If we know how important focus, collaborative inquiry that challenges thinking and practice, and instructional leadership are in terms of enabling professional learning, why can't we just get on with it? You're probably thinking, "Fine, real new learning is hard. But we know what's important in terms of creating the conditions for it. So let's start learning!" We wish that's all there was to it. But like most things that are worthwhile, the road less travelled is a bumpy one. And the bumps come packaged as an implementation challenge. The reason we don't see nearly as much of the kind of professional learning that changes practices as we'd hope is because implementation isn't only about putting the enablers in place; it's also about removing barriers.

Take a look back at Figure 1.2 in Chapter 1. The three key enablers that we've talked about in this chapter sit as islands in a sea of barriers. We briefly mentioned one of these barriers earlier in this chapter— the imposter syndrome. The imposter syndrome impedes real new learning because it makes you stay quiet rather than ask questions and open your practice up for scrutiny and challenge. It inhibits shape-sorter opportunities. But challenge, as we've said before, isn't an unfortunate consequence of new learning; it's an essential prerequisite for it that requires intentionally interrupting the imposter syndrome. We've highlighted one strategy for doing so in terms of visible and public colearning on the part of leaders. The imposter syndrome, however, is but one example of a barrier that needs to be intentionally interrupted. In Chapter 5, we describe a number of other influential barriers, and in Chapter 6, we take a look at strategies for intentionally interrupting them.

Time for Reflection

Take some time to consider the following questions:

- Does your school have a professional learning focus (using the criteria for focus outlined in this chapter)? Is there a student learning need that defines the teacher learning need that defines the leader learning need? What are the identified learning needs at each of these levels, and how do they align?
- Look back at the inquiry cycle outlined in this chapter. Which, if any, components of this cycle are evident in your professional learning environment, and which are missing?
- If you are in a formal leadership position, would you consider yourself to be a lead learner? Why or why not?

5

The Barriers:
How Our Minds
Get in the Way

Introduction

We ended Chapter 4 by making reference to a critical implementation challenge around embedding (and sustaining) the key enablers of real professional learning. We referred back to Figure 1.2 in Chapter 1 in illustration of the barriers that the enablers are embedded within and that need to be intentionally interrupted. This chapter describes these psychological barriers, or obstacles, and the forms that they often take in a professional learning setting. In order to get to real professional learning, people need to learn to navigate their way through the barriers, and this requires intentional facilitation. Remember, facilitation is not about a particular person, but it is about a particular role. And the role is to intentionally interrupt the barriers that get in the way of learning.

Barriers to Learning: What Needs to Be Interrupted?

At their core, all of the barriers to successfully enabling real professional learning are premised on one fairly simple (yet often hard to believe) fact: *Human beings take mental shortcuts to avoid thinking.* And moreover, *all* human beings (you included!) use these mental shortcuts. In fact, humans have evolved to take these shortcuts and to do the least amount of thinking possible. Psychologists, biologists, and cognitive scientists have explained this evolutionary foundation in terms of the need to simplify things (like the amount of information that we are continuously faced with) in order to survive. Historically, quick decisions ensured survival, and lower-order thinking solutions tend to be faster than higher-order ones (Dattner & Dahl, 2011; Stanovich, 2009; Willingham, 2009). Human beings have evolved into what Stanovich (2009) describes as "cognitive misers." We tend to think as little as we can. By being human, we are wired to avoid deep thinking and take the easy way out as much as possible. Our natural tendency is actually to be lazy when it comes to hard thinking.

In Chapter 2, we described people's natural inclination to respond to the experience of challenge by either avoiding it altogether or trying to turn something novel into something familiar so that the feeling of challenge dissipates. Despite the fact that everyone does this, most people believe that they are the exception. In fact, research shows that most people believe that they do more thinking than the average person. As Gilbert (2006) writes, "If you are like most people, then like most people, you don't know you're like most people" (p. 229). This is especially important to realize as you read the rest of this chapter. Despite the almost certain fact that you will believe something to the contrary, you are *not* an exception. Everyone falls prey to the thinking errors that we describe in this chapter, and neither intelligence nor level of education does much to guard against them. Stanovich (2009) has shown that thinking errors are not prevented by having a high IQ, because rational decision making is not typically included in people's definition of what it means to be "smart," and IQ tests fail to measure these kinds of thinking skills. In fact, people who are more intelligent may actually be worse off when it comes to these kinds of thinking errors because they're better at rationalizing why they are committing them. As Wansink (2011) put it, "Intelligent people especially can figure out a rationalization for anything they want to believe. We call it the intelligence trap" (p. 6).

The fact that intelligence does not protect against these biases and thinking errors (and perhaps even makes them worse) is critical to recognize because, as you read on, you will almost certainly say something like, "This sounds like a lot of other people I know, but not me. I wouldn't do these things, I'm smarter than that." We're not saying that you're not intelligent, but we are saying that you are human. And as a human, you need to understand that this chapter is first and foremost about you. Let's take a closer look at some of the biases that make smart people (like you and like us) avoid deep levels of thinking.

We Don't Think Through All Possibilities

Consider the following scenario that unfolded at an elementary school we had occasion to visit: The school has an established professional learning community (PLC) that works together on a particular professional learning focus—descriptive feedback. On the day that we visited, we arrived at the meeting room where the principal and the school's three Grade 7 teachers were gathered. The group was preparing to do a "walkthrough" of the Grade 1 classrooms. We were told that the purpose of the walkthrough was to look at what the Grade 1 teachers were doing with respect to descriptive feedback. The Grade 7 teachers told us about the work that they had done up front (in a prior meeting) to prepare for the day's walkthrough, which included identifying the purpose of the walkthrough and establishing a set of "look-fors." It was evident that the walkthrough was anchored in some kind of bigger purpose. Since we weren't privy to the background context, one of us asked the principal how the walkthrough came about, which she explained as follows:

> I was recently at a network meeting with my principal colleagues [this principal works with a group of other principals in a learning network]. During the meeting, I was describing my current "problem of practice" as an instructional leader in my school. I told my colleagues that I am having difficulty getting the intermediate teachers in my school on board with the learning focus [descriptive feedback] and that, from my perspective, the problem is that my teachers don't actually understand what descriptive feedback looks like. So, one of my colleagues said to me, "I had the exact same problem last year, and you know what fixed it for me? When I had my intermediate teachers go visit my Grade 1 class and see what they were doing with regards to descriptive feedback. Somehow seeing that the Grade 1 teachers could do it with such young children inspired the intermediate teachers to think about changing their own practice, and the excitement and motivation really caught on from there." And so I thought to myself, "What a great idea, I bet that would work in my school!" So I asked my colleague some questions about how she organized the visit so I could try to do the same. Then I came back to my school and suggested this to the Grade 7

teachers. They were a bit reluctant but eventually agreed to do it. We had a meeting last week to prepare for today, as they were telling you about, and they seemed to get more enthusiastic. So, here we are today. I'm hoping that I have the same success that my colleague had, because my intermediate teachers are really lagging behind the other divisions when it comes to descriptive feedback.

Hearing this explanation made us wonder if this walkthrough really was the right strategy for this principal and the group of teachers that we were with that day. How did the principal know that what the Grade 7 teachers needed was to see what descriptive feedback looks like in Grade 1? Did she consider other possibilities for what might be behind the reluctance of the Grade 7 teachers to learn about descriptive feedback? What if the root of the problem in her school was not that the intermediate teachers didn't know what descriptive feedback looks like, as she hypothesized, but was actually that these teachers didn't believe that descriptive feedback is important or that they didn't think they had anything to learn about descriptive feedback (or a number of other possibilities)?

It's not that we're saying that this walkthrough was the wrong activity for the Grade 7 teachers in this school to be engaging in. In fact, if the principal was correct in her hypothesis, then the walkthrough may have been just what those teachers needed. What we are saying, however, is that this is a good illustration of the tendency that people have to commit to decisions or solutions or actions without really unpacking the problem and considering all the possible avenues of approach. We alluded to this human tendency in Chapter 3 when we explained our own rationale for unpacking the "problem" of professional learning in some detail, before starting to talk about possible ways forward. This principal seemed not to spend much time unpacking her problem of practice and was quite quick to adopt the strategy used by her colleague, without taking the time to really consider her own situation. As we said earlier, the walkthrough strategy was anchored in an inquiry (which is a good thing), but what if the inquiry was the wrong question for the particular problem of practice? In that case, the walkthrough starts to feel like an activity trap—valuable time spent on something well intentioned, but not needs based (Katz, Earl, & Ben Jaafar, 2009).

Human beings tend not to be particularly good at thinking through all possible angles when considering a problem. We tend to jump to action very quickly, and educators are no exception. Most people don't spend enough time trying to unpack their "problems of practice" and really understand them prior to committing to a course of action. Most educators are "action people," who like to feel that they are getting something accomplished and so often take shortcuts in the problem analysis. But this becomes a problem, as in the example above. Had this principal spent longer describing her problem of practice to her network colleagues, as well as thinking through all the possible ways to proceed, something more suitable may have arisen. People often feel as if spending all that time up front is a waste when it could be better used to actually implement a course of action. This principal, for example, was likely feeling as if she needed to get moving on "fixing" the problem so that the practice of descriptive feedback in the intermediate division could move forward.

The principal in our example is not alone in her failure to engage in a thorough problem analysis. In fact, the human tendency to commit to decisions without spending enough time identifying the problem is linked to a cognitive bias that everyone carries. Consider the following scenario (Levesque, 1989), popular in the cognitive reasoning literature:

Jack is looking at Ann, but Ann is looking at George. Jack is married, but George is not. Is a married person looking at an unmarried person?

A. Yes

B. No

C. Cannot be determined

Think of your own response to this problem before looking at the solution below. Answer either A, B, or C.

Toplak and Stanovich (2002) found that only 13% of participants answer this question correctly on the first try. The vast majority of people choose option C (cannot be determined). The reasoning behind choosing option C is that we don't know whether or not Ann is married, and she is involved in both scenarios (Jack is looking at Ann and Ann is looking at George), so how could we know if a married person is looking at an unmarried person? This reasoning is actually incorrect. If you are surprised to read this, you are not alone. This is the reasoning used by most people who see this problem for the first time. The correct answer is actually option A—we know that a married person is looking at an unmarried person. This is because Ann can only be either married or unmarried. If Ann is married, then we know that a married person is looking at an unmarried person when Ann is looking at George (because we've already been told that George is unmarried). If Ann is unmarried then we know that a married person is looking at an unmarried person when Jack is looking at Ann (because we've already been told that Jack is married). So regardless of whether Ann is married or not, we can conclusively answer that yes, a married person is looking at an unmarried person.

Once someone explains the reasoning behind the correct answer, most people quickly understand and may even feel slightly silly for not answering that way in the first place. But as we've already said, over 85% of people answer this problem incorrectly on the first try. Why is this? Because human beings are quite poor at thinking through all possible options when making a decision, which is called disjunctive reasoning. It is not a natural tendency to think about the fact that there are only two choices for Ann's marital status and to think through what the implications of each would be. You might be wondering what a brain teaser like this has to do with the reality of the challenges of professional learning in schools, which are so much more complex. But that's exactly the point. In this situation, there are only two possible options for Ann's marital status (married or not married), yet people are still not good at thinking through the possibilities. So imagine how difficult it is when there are many more options, as there are in the scenario we described above, about the Grade 7 teachers and descriptive feedback.

Everyone takes mental shortcuts in order to get moving on doing the work. But interrupting this natural propensity for failing to really understand the problems or challenges at sufficient depth is crucial because it's the best strategy for avoiding activity traps. As we mentioned in Chapter 3, the expertise literature shows that experts are faster than novices at all stages of problem solving, save one—the problem analysis stage, in which they actually spend a significantly larger proportion of their time. Experts spend a long time mapping out the requirements of a problem before committing to action (Glaser & Chi, 1988). When people act like experts, they realize the value of spending time up front to really map out the problem and a range of potential solutions. One way of doing this is to interrupt the cognitive bias of failing to think through all possible options before committing to an action.

We Focus on *Confirming* Our Hypotheses, Not Challenging Them

Another cognitive bias that is rampant for humans is what's known as the *confirmation bias*. The confirmation bias refers to the idea that, once people have a hypothesis about something, they tend to look only for things that confirm rather than challenge it. Numerous researchers have found evidence of the confirmation bias in adults (e.g., Evans & Feeney, 2004; Legrenzi, Girotto, & Johnson-Laird, 1993; Shafir, 1994), and the confirmation bias has even been examined in children as young as three years of age (e.g., Bucciarelli and Johnson-Laird, 2001; Cummins, 1996; Dack, 2008). What the confirmation bias essentially shows is that people tend to engage with the world in a way that confirms what they already think, believe, know, and do, and work hard to avoid evidence to the contrary.

Wason (1966), a well-known thinking and reasoning researcher, told a group of people something along the lines of the following: "I have a rule in mind that describes sets of three whole numbers. 2–4–6 is a set of three numbers that conforms to my rule. Try to figure out what my rule is. Come up with your own sets of three numbers and ask me if they conform to the rule, and then try to guess the rule from there." In truth, the "rule" that Wason had in mind was "any ascending sequence of numbers," but of course, the participant doesn't know this. Most people's initial hypothesis (which may have been yours as well) is that the rule is that each number goes up by two, or that there is an equal interval between the numbers. As such, people tend to start guessing things like 10–12–14 (increasing by two) or 100–500–900 (increasing at equal intervals), both of which conform to the rule they have in mind (their hypothesis). What's important to note here is that people tend to test their hypotheses using only positive examples (i.e., examples that they believe conform to the rule). And what they rarely do is test examples that they think might *not* conform to the rule, and so they never receive disconfirming evidence. As such, they become more and more convinced that their original hypothesis is correct. If they simply chose an example like 1–2–5 (a guess that they would expect to *not* conform to the rule), they would be told that this is also correct and would quickly realize that their initial hypothesis was wrong. But people tend not to think that way. We don't try to prove ourselves wrong; we try to support what we already think. As a result, we often don't get the kind of disconfirming evidence that would lead us to change our beliefs.

You might be wondering if you fall prey to the confirmation bias, and again, we would say that you likely do. You're human after all. A recent example of the confirmation bias came to us in a secondary school PLC meeting that we attended as critical friends. At this particular meeting, a group of teachers was engaged in a professional reading activity where they all read the same professional article and then had a discussion about it. After the teachers had each read the article and were ready to begin the discussion, we asked each of them to show us their articles that they had highlighted and marked up (as many of us do when we read). We also asked each of them to explain *why* they had highlighted or underlined the particular parts of the article that they had. What we found was that people were almost exclusively highlighting the parts of the article that said the things that they already believed to be true (often emphasized by asterisks and exclamation marks in the margin) and tended not to highlight those parts that challenged their current thoughts, beliefs, and practices. Take a look at the last professional article that you read and marked up and see if this is true for you. Is there a sentence that you highlighted in yellow, put an asterisk and an exclamation mark beside, and underlined in red ink? What sentence is it? Probably one that supports your current way of thinking but articulates it in a really eloquent way! Do you have any sentences highlighted that challenge your existing beliefs or practices? In reality, things that challenge us and make us uncomfortable are the parts that we tend to read quickly or skim and tend not to be ones that we focus our attention on.

This is an example of the confirmation bias at work. We start with a particular belief or idea and then (subconsciously) look for evidence that confirms it rather than challenges it. This is problematic because the things that challenge current ways of thinking are the ones that often lead to real new learning. Think back to the examples we provided in Chapter 2 when we illustrated how learning really happens. Remember the example that we gave about moderated marking of the persuasive writing essay? Imagine yourself in a situation like that. If you go into a moderated marking session like the one we described saying, "I already know that this is good persuasive writing," then you'll probably only look for evidence that confirms that belief. If your colleague presents you with disconfirming evidence, you'll likely either ignore it or try to change it to fit with your beliefs. In essence, you'll avoid the challenge and try to focus on what confirms your existing hypothesis. And this is what we need to intentionally interrupt. Because as in that example in Chapter 2, it is only when you encounter *disconfirming* evidence (i.e., "But where is the part of this essay where the student is trying to convince the reader?") that you become aware of the limitation of your existing understandings.

The confirmation bias runs in the background, at a subconscious level, all the time. People see the world through the lens of what they currently think, believe, know, and do, and they constantly look for evidence to support the status quo. It's the reason why, as we said earlier, opposites don't really attract, but birds of a feather do flock together. When people have a choice, they surround themselves with people who are "like them" and who tell them what they want to hear. And they avoid people (when they have a choice) who challenge them. But without challenge, from people or from artifacts, they can't really learn. Learning is about making a permanent change in thinking or behavior. So without change, there is no learning. Interrupting the confirmation bias forces people to engage with evidence that might contradict current ways of thinking and believing.

We Pay Too Much Attention to Things That Are Vivid

Have you ever heard the following: "Adoption increases the chance of an infertile couple getting pregnant naturally"? Most people have heard this, and many of them can tell you a story of someone they know (or know *of*) that this happened to. The supporting rationale is something like once the pressure is off and the couple is less anxious, it will happen naturally. However, it turns out that there is no empirical evidence that this is true. Research has shown that the percentage of women who become pregnant after adopting is no different than the percentage of women who become pregnant without adopting (Resolve, n.d.). What this means is that, while a small percentage of people who were having difficulty getting pregnant do get pregnant after adopting a child, these are likely the same people who would have gotten pregnant after having difficulty, even without the adoption. It has nothing to do with the adoption.

So why do so many people believe this myth? Because of what we've said above; many people can tell you a story of someone they know that this happened to. But the thing is, most people can only tell you *one* story. And they don't tell you all the stories they know about the infertile couples that adopted a child and *didn't* get pregnant naturally afterward. The examples of where it did happen are salient to them, perhaps because they remember thinking to themselves, "This couple is going to have two babies within a few months of age of each other!" What happens when something is salient—or we when it produces a vivid memory—is that people tend to overemphasize the likelihood of its occurrence. And they give it a lot of attention. This is known as the *vividness bias*. The vividness bias is supported by what's often referred to as an illusory correlation—the impression that two variables are related when in fact they are not. In our adoption/pregnancy example, because of one or two very salient or vivid examples, many people believe that there is a relationship between adoption and getting pregnant, when in reality, there is not. Other popular examples of the illusory correlation include "the phone always rings when I get in the shower" or "it always rains on the weekends." In these examples, people tend to focus on the times when these things have happened and don't think about all the times when they didn't. They remember those times when the phone rang when they were in the shower (likely because it's annoying) but don't think about all the times the phone rang when they were not in the shower. In reality, the phone is no more likely to ring when they're in the shower than when they are not, but they tend to believe there's a relationship between being in the shower and the phone ringing because of the vividness of the examples in which it has happened.

So how does this vividness bias play out in the context of professional learning? We recently experienced the vividness bias at work with a group of principals who were working together in a leader learning network. The learning focus for this group of principals was on how to effectively embed and support PLCs in their schools. At a recent meeting, there was significant conversation among the principals on how to deal with "resisters" on staff. All the principals were struggling with this, and they spent the majority of the meeting trying to figure out what changes to make to their in-school PLC meetings to deal with it. After the conversation had been going on for over an hour, with significant talk about revamping the PLC structure in the schools, the group took a break. During the break, the one of us who was present asked one of the principals how many individuals the group was talking about: how many staff members would be described as resisters. The response was, "This group of schools has a big problem with that. Each of us has a substantial number of resisters." When the meeting reconvened, we asked the same question to the group, asking them to make a list and count the number of staff in their schools that they were talking about. And what emerged is that on an average staff of about thirty, there tended to be two or three resisters. In reality that's not very many, yet over an hour was spent on this topic as *the* major problem of practice, and more importantly, principals were talking about changing the way they run PLCs with their entire staffs to respond to it. Let us make clear that we are not saying that the principals didn't need a strategy for dealing with the resisters or that it was a fruitless discussion. Figuring out how to work with resisters is crucial, even if they're small in number. But this was an example of the vividness bias at play because the principals were overrepresenting these few individuals and were developing an entire change management strategy based on them, when what they really needed was a differentiated strategy (one for the two or three resisters and another for all the other staff). The resisters are vivid because their resistance is likely overt; perhaps, they are the few individuals who are always complaining or making negative comments, and so they're noticeable and memorable. And because these instances and experiences are so vivid, the principals ended up believing that there were more resisters than there really were, and they were prepared to make consequential decisions on that basis.

The vividness bias also plays out in professional learning through what is known as the *recognition heuristic*, which says that people place greater value on things that they recognize than on things that they don't. And this sometimes means that they value the wrong things and, in turn, make poorer decisions than they otherwise might. In some interesting British research cited by Stanovich (2009), MacErlean (2002) looked at the banking institutions in which people were choosing to put their money. This research found that 70% of the people asked had their money in bank accounts in one of the four banks that were the most well known in Britain, despite the fact that substantially better rates were available from other, less well-known places. Essentially, people were choosing to put their money in a bank that they recognized and was vivid to them, even if it wasn't really in their best interest (pun intended)!

But how does this apply to professional learning? It applies because educators often place a high value on ideas, strategies, or resources that are well known. We're not saying that this in and of itself is problematic. The problem arises when teachers and administrators look to particular strategies simply *because* they're well known, but not because they're fit for purpose. And as a result, they would likely ignore strategies they've never heard of, and they may miss the opportunity to learn from a strategy or resource that better applies to their particular problem of practice. As we will see in Chapter 6, purpose is paramount when it comes to choosing the right tools for the job. It is important to intentionally interrupt the vividness bias and its sidekick—the recognition heuristic—and learn to lead with need and focus on tools and strategies that are well suited for the job.

We Consider Ourselves to Be Exceptions

This is a big one. And it's one that we've already described earlier in this chapter; we just didn't name it. Remember our warning to you at the beginning of this chapter not to let yourself believe that the things we're talking about here don't apply to you? We mentioned that the first inclination when anyone hears about these cognitive biases is to think, "This sounds like many other people I know, but not me." There's a cognitive bias at work here. It has been referred to by different names, but the one we like best is *illusory superiority*. The idea behind the illusory superiority bias is that people tend to overestimate their own strengths and underestimate their shortcomings, in comparison to other people. Cognitive biases are essentially mental shortcomings, which is why when people hear about them, they believe they apply to other people and not themselves. Research has found that although people do recognize that the biases in thinking and judgment described in the chapter exist, they tend to believe that they are exceptions (see, for example, Pronin, 2006). Dattner and Dahl (2011) explain illusory superiority by using the example of the way people assign credit and blame. That is, most people believe that they deserve more credit for something than they would be willing to give someone else who has done the exact same thing. And on the flipside, they tend to assign themselves less blame than they would to someone else who has done the same thing.

Most people are guilty of this pattern of thinking and behavior. When someone else makes a mistake, we are quicker to blame them than we would be to accept the blame if we made the same mistake. For example, if someone else fails a test, the conjecture might be they didn't study hard enough. But if we fail the test, the response is more likely that the test was really difficult or that we were having a bad day. Again, people see themselves as the exception to the general rule, and because of that, they're often unwilling to take responsibility for their actions. Sullivan (2010) describes the human reluctance to take responsibility for their own less-than-stellar performances, referring to the tennis player who hits a bad shot and immediately looks at the strings on his racquet or the dancer who falls and immediately checks her shoelaces. And we can all think of the example of the teacher whose lesson doesn't go as well as planned and heads into the staffroom afterward to complain that her students were "not on" that day.

So how does this relate to professional learning? Illusory superiority impacts on professional learning because it makes people less likely to feel like they "need to know." It's not that they don't want to learn; they often don't believe that they *need* to learn anything new. It's not uncommon for teachers to say (either outwardly or privately to themselves), "My practice is fine. I'm not the one who needs to make a change, but other people do." But we know that teachers' practice isn't always "fine." Our discussion about the concept of a needs-based learning focus in the last chapter made that clear. In addition, even when teachers do engage with their colleagues under the guise of collaborative inquiry, illusory superiority plays a role. Think about yourself. Do you have an easier time *giving* professional feedback than receiving it? Most of us do! But impactful collaborative inquiry involves *both* challenging and being challenged. People need to understand that they are likely not very different from those around them. As such, illusory superiority is another barrier to intentionally interrupt.

We Hesitate to Take Action in a New Direction

Most people consider harm that results from the actions they've taken to be worse than harm resulting from not taking any action, which is called the *omission bias*. But is that really the case? For example, if you actively do something to hurt someone else, it tends to be thought of as worse than if you fail to stop someone from being hurt. In both cases, however, the person has gotten hurt, and you had a hand in it. One domain in which the omission bias is regularly discussed in the literature is in investigating the controversial parental decision around immunizing their children. In some cases, parents are so fearful about the harm that could come about from immunizing a child that they choose not to do it, even though the risk of harm from immunization is significantly lower than the risk of harm from the disease against which you're immunizing. For example, one study (see Ritov & Baron, 1990) found that some parents opposed immunization when the risk of death from the disease in question (influenza) was 10 in 10,000 and risk of death from immunization was 5 in 10,000 (and, of course, the vaccination eliminates the chance of contracting the disease). In essence, this cognitive bias plays out in the fact that people somehow feel that harm caused by taking action is worse than harm caused by taking no action.

The reason that this bias is so important to understand—and to intentionally interrupt—is because it makes people risk averse. They are so afraid of the potential downside of action that they sometimes choose inaction. What people fail to grasp is that doing nothing is, in fact, doing something. There is no such thing as nothing. Nothing is what they are currently doing; it's a choice to preserve the status quo. Let's say, for example, that a teacher is being encouraged to change the way she teaches literacy, perhaps by rebalancing her program, to try to meet the needs of the students in her classroom. She's afraid to take the risk and make the change because the change could make things worse for her students. She believes that doing nothing and staying the course is risk neutral. But doing nothing isn't really doing nothing—it's doing *nothing new.* And doing nothing new isn't risk neutral if she's already failing to meet the needs of some of her students, which prompted the suggestion to change in the first place. The omission bias, as you can see, impedes real new learning.

We often see the omission bias at work in the context of professional learning when we work with teachers and administrators to narrow their professional learning foci—to trade breadth for depth, or as we said in the previous chapter, to identify the "right inch." When we talk to educators about the need to identify a learning focus, they are often afraid to commit to something narrow. They say things like, "Right now, I'm part of a book study about improving student confidence in math, and I just attended workshop on writing tests, and I'm working with my grade partner on joint assignments around narrative writing. I'm learning about a whole bunch of different things that can make a difference for kids. Why would I need (or want) to focus on just one?" People consider it risky to narrow the professional learning focus. They believe that if they take this action (identify a narrow learning focus) and harm is done (their students fail to improve), it is more problematic than if they stay the course (continue to work on many things at once) and harm is done (their students fail to improve). But in reality, the risk associated with staying the course may be worse than the risk associated with narrowing the focus. What people often don't realize is that if their students (some or all) are currently failing to improve, then harm is already being done. Again, doing nothing is never really doing nothing—it's continuing to do what is currently being done, which already comes with risk. Identifying and moving forward with a needs-based learning focus is about realizing the inherent risk in maintaining the status quo. It's why the omission bias needs to be intentionally interrupted.

We Don't Want Others to See Our Vulnerabilities

It's important for most people to appear to others as if they know what they're doing. We try to maximize our strengths and minimize our weaknesses, and we try to present the strongest version of ourselves to the outside world. This likely has an evolutionary basis, in that strength was linked to survival. As such, most human beings try very hard to avoid others seeing areas in which they might be weak or vulnerable. This can manifest in a number of different ways. First, because they don't want people to see their weaknesses, they often fail to reach out for help even if they know they need it. This regularly happens in the professional learning environment. In the previous chapter, we described the imposter syndrome—the little voice that we all carry around with us that says, "I have no idea how I came to be where I am, but hopefully, nobody will find me out." And as we said before, while everybody has this feeling, people often believe that they're the only ones who do. The net effect is that people keep their questions to themselves and work hard to hide their vulnerabilities (real or imagined). Many people express the need to "deprivatize practice" as one of the biggest challenges within a PLC. And sometimes the reference to "hiding" is literal—like when teachers cover the little window of glass on their doors with brown paper! It's not only teachers; we see it with administrators at all levels as well. Many principals that we have worked with have described scenarios where they have been involved in professional dialogue and have been confused or in need of clarification but too afraid to speak up and expose the fact that they "don't know." This becomes a missed learning opportunity.

Sometimes the need to appear knowledgeable manifests in a stubbornness around "being right." Most people prefer to be right rather than wrong: to be the one that comes out ahead in an argument, be it professional or personal. They forget that the goal is to deepen understanding. They think it's about winning, about being right. In the context of our shape-sorter analogy, it's the child who cannot accept that the triangle won't fit in the circular hole (leading to an understanding that shapes are different) and instead does everything possible to hammer it in, even breaking the toy in the process. When being wrong is seen as a weakness, it gets in the way of learning. If people don't allow themselves to admit that they may have been wrong or that someone else's idea or perspective is important, how can they expect to end up with any real new learning?

This has implications for how to conceptualize mistakes, which are more often thought of as windows to our vulnerabilities than opportunities for new learning. As Tugend (2011) writes, despite the fact that everyone is told from childhood that they need to make mistakes in order to learn, in reality, they are often punished for them. There's that song that Big Bird sings on Sesame Street that goes like this: "Oh everyone makes mistakes, oh yes they do. Your sister and your brother and your mother and father too. . . ." Big Bird sings that if you get stuck while trying to count to ten, it's okay and you should just start over or get some help, and if you spill a glass of milk, your parents will still like you as much as before because they too spilled milk when they were small. The messages in this song are the same ones that people are told throughout childhood and into adulthood: You won't be penalized for mistakes, and there are people around you who will help you improve when you make them. Sometimes we are even told that mistakes help us learn or grow—hence the saying "learn from our mistakes"—and that we need to make them to get better. The problem is that, for most people, this is just rhetoric, and the gap between saying and doing is a wide one.

The reality is that both children and adults are often penalized for mistakes. Despite words to the contrary, children, both in school and at home, often receive consequences for the mistakes they make, rather than being encouraged to focus on problem solving and on improvement in the future. The child who spills his milk is told it's okay but is given a cup with a lid the next time, "just to make sure you don't spill again." And the adult who makes a mistake in the workplace may be told not to worry, that the mistake is a way to learn, but may find that when a similar task comes along again, it's given to someone else. And adults, both within and outside the workplace, spend more time blaming others for mistakes and separating themselves from them, rather than trying to find a solution. This creates a culture where mistakes are not really seen as functional. When push comes to shove, most people don't really believe that mistakes are an integral part of new learning. And so they make sure to avoid them by protecting and perpetuating the status quo. This propensity must be intentionally interrupted in order to enable real professional learning.

Coming Together in a Culture of "Niceness"

Taken together, you can see how the biases described above mitigate against defining a narrow professional learning focus, against a collaborative inquiry process that *challenges* thinking and practice in ourselves and others, and against a conception of instructional leadership framed in terms of a lead learner rather than a lead knower. The biases impede the key enablers of real professional learning, and they contribute to maintaining the status quo. This status quo can be described as a culture of "niceness" (Elmore, 2007), though in this case being "nice" really means being superficial. In the culture of niceness, beliefs, ideas, and practices are superficially validated in collaborative exchanges (at least publicly), and opportunities for critical challenge that lead to deep understanding (accommodation) are exceptionally rare. Moreover, in the culture of niceness, person and practice are seen as one in the same. Challenging the practice means challenging the person, so it doesn't happen. Creating the conditions for real new learning means pulling person and practice apart. It means intentionally interrupting the culture of niceness and the biases that you've read about in this chapter that support it. The question of how to do that is unpacked in Chapter 6.

Time for Reflection

Consider the following questions:

- Think of your last problem of professional practice. How did you respond to this problem? Thinking back on it now, did you engage in appropriate "problem analysis" before implementing your response? Did your response work? How do you know? Is there anything you might do differently if you were in the same situation again?
- As you read the example about the PLC meeting and highlighting points of agreement in the article (in relation to the confirmation bias), what were you thinking? Did the idea of the confirmation bias resonate with you? Can you think of a time when you have recently fallen prey to the confirmation bias? What were the implications of this?
- What is the culture around mistakes in your school or in the schools that you work with? What is your own view on making mistakes?
- Think back to how you answered the reflection questions about focus, collaborative inquiry, and leadership at the end of Chapter 4. Do you see any links between your responses to those questions and the biases you've read about in this chapter?

6

Intentional Interruption

Introduction

Up until now, this book has been defining the problem of professional learning, and we've tried to do this in some depth. Earlier on, we referenced the literature on expertise and underscored the importance of spending significant time and effort unpacking the challenge at hand—in our case, the challenge of professional learning. We've seen that even when people think professional learning is a sure thing, it isn't. Even when the most committed among us set out to enable it in ways that they know matter, they often fall short. People's minds get in the way. Real learning remains elusive and is replaced with activity. So what do we do? How do we facilitate the kind of professional learning that has real learning (a permanent change in thinking and practice) at its heart? What does it mean to *intentionally interrupt* the biases that we described in Chapter 5?

The first step of interruption is recognizing that, within your reality, there are some things that you can have direct control over and some things that you can't. Most people don't have much influence over things such as who the students in the school are, who else is on staff, the broader district context of what's being prioritized, or the broader political context in which the education system is situated. Although most people recognize that they can't really control these things, many still put significant time and energy toward thinking about how much they wish they could. This is an activity trap. We have such limited time to work on improvement; we might as well spend it in places where we actually have the most control. So instead of sitting around and wishing you could change the things that aren't in your control, focus on the things that are in your control and where you can put your efforts toward changing. This is a much more empowering attitude, one that will lead you to actually take action.

This chapter focuses on strategies for interrupting the cognitive biases that get in the way of enabling professional learning. The list is not exhaustive, and some of the strategies may not apply to you, at least not at the given moment. But what's important to understand is that the strategies described here are all within your control; they are all things that you can intentionally do to interrupt the barriers that impede real learning.

Strategies for Interruption

Behavioral scientists make the distinction between tasks that are algorithmic and tasks that are heuristic. The former are things that allow you to follow a set of established instructions down a single pathway to one conclusion. The latter require that you experiment with possibilities and devise novel approaches because there is no algorithm. Although it might appear otherwise, the strategies that we describe in this chapter are heuristic, not algorithmic. It isn't possible to match biases to strategies in a one-to-one relationship. Intentionally interrupting the biases asks for adaptive expertise (for example, see Hatano & Oura, 2003). You need to understand how the biases work (as articulated in Chapter 5), and you need to think about the strategies discussed in this chapter as heuristics that you can draw on if, when, and how you need them. You don't work through the strategies as a chronological "to do" list.

The analogy we like to use is shopping for tools at the hardware store. You don't typically walk into the hardware store and say to the salesperson, "I'm looking for a tool. Any tool will do. I just want it to be new and something I can use." Instead, you go in and describe the problem you're experiencing (what it is that you're trying to do) and then work with the salesperson to determine which tool will help solve that problem; it's often a tool you didn't even know existed. Starting with the tool doesn't make any sense. That would be like giving a five-year-old a hammer. Everything starts to look like a nail! You'd rather start with a nail that needs to be knocked in and then decide that the hammer may be the way to go. It's the same for the strategies described in this chapter. You need to start with your problem of practice and determine which tool or strategy will best meet that need, that is, which one will give you the best chance at interrupting the status quo and enabling a different way of moving forward. And we need to guard against the risk of using strategies just because they're there and because they make us feel busy. That's an activity trap all over again.

One of our biggest concerns with some of the school districts that we work in is that, when it comes to professional learning, they often seem to be in the tool business rather than the learning business. Sometimes fidelity to the process of using the tool trumps the learning that it was intended to enable. Success gets defined (and measured) based on how many tools have been used, how many people/schools have used them, and whether people have followed the instructions correctly (i.e., implementation). But that doesn't mean that any learning has happened! Therefore, it's critical that the strategies you read about here don't get interpreted as the "it" of professional learning, but instead, as tools to help get at the "it" (i.e., the learning). With that caution in mind, let's take a closer look at some of the ways we might intentionally interrupt the barriers that get in the way of true professional learning. And remember, they're not algorithms!

Using Protocols

Protocols are structured sets of guidelines to promote effective and efficient communication and problem solving, and they offer a useful application of procedural knowledge to the work of professional learning. There are a host of different kinds of protocols out there, and this isn't intended to be a book about protocols, but from our perspective, the purpose of using any of these is essentially the same: Protocols help focus on the task at hand, and they help to mitigate the impact of some of the barriers described in the previous chapter. For example, we talked at the end of Chapter 5 about the culture of "niceness" in schools and the difficulty that people tend to have separating person from practice. When providing feedback to one another, people tend to avoid any kind of comment that could be interpreted as negative or challenging because of a belief that this kind of feedback isn't "nice" because it takes issue with the person's value as a professional. Alternatively, when there is some kind of constructive feedback to provide, it gets coupled with a superficially positive comment to maintain the facade of "niceness." Protocols help to interrupt this propensity to avoid challenge, by providing step-by-step instructions on how to describe practice and provide feedback on it in a way that separates person from practice.

As we said, there are many different kinds of protocols out there, and there are entire books that have been written to describe all the different choices and the particular scenarios in which they work best (e.g., Easton, 2009; McDonald, Mohr, Dichter, & McDonald, 2007). For example, there are protocols to explore a problem of practice, assess whether an assignment meets a teacher's goals, look at student work samples, help teachers determine what and how students are thinking, provide feedback on a teacher's assignment, and many others. From our perspective, protocols don't need to be fancy or overly complicated in their instructions; what they need to do (and this is why we like them) is provide a structure that forces people to do things that they wouldn't naturally do, like separate person from practice and/or description from interpretation. It's usually a good idea, with protocols, for someone to take responsibility for leading or facilitating the process (e.g., forcing people to stick to the instructions and complete each step, stick to the timelines, stop inappropriate discourse, etc.).

Table 6.1 is an example of a protocol (adapted from Little and Curry, 2008) that we have used with groups of administrators who are trying to deepen their understanding of the assessment and evaluation practices used by teachers in their schools. The protocol helps administrators describe and interpret teachers' feedback practices and is used when looking at samples of student work that include written comments by the teacher (which is taken as evidence of teacher practice and understanding). You will see that the protocol is not complicated, but it does outline a set of steps to complete so that the parts of the process that don't come naturally to people don't get skipped. In the first step of this protocol, the leader/facilitator reviews the sequence and time limits for anyone new to the process and reviews the norms for behavior (e.g., following the steps, not placing blame, etc.). Following this, the presenting administrator presents the piece of assessed student work that he or she wants the group to look at. The presenter is asked to only give as much information as is required to introduce the piece of work, not to tell a long story about the school improvement process in his or her school (which often turns out to be the case in the absence of the protocol that stipulates only two minutes for this step). In the second step, the group describes the teacher work that they see in front of them (in this case the teacher work is the written comments on the assignment, along with any grade, etc.), without interpretation (description only) and without interruption from the presenter. For example, someone might say, "I notice that this teacher has used a lot of comments like

Table 6.1   Teacher Feedback Analysis Protocol

Protocol Step	Instructions
Introduction (2 min)	• Leader to review process and norms (follow the steps, no placing blame, collaboration) • Presenter to give a very brief explanation of the assignment and show the teacher work
Describing the teacher work (10 min)	• The group gathers as much information as possible about the work and describes what they see (no judgements or interpretation of what the teacher was doing).
Interpreting the teacher work (10 min)	• The group tries to make sense of what the teacher was doing and why. It tries to figure out what the teacher was thinking, does/does not understand, was most interested in, and how he or she interpreted the assignment. • Seek out as many interpretations as possible
Implications for practice (10 min)	• The group discusses implications for teaching and assessment in the classroom based on their observations and interpretations.
Discussing next steps (5 min)	• The presenting principal summarizes what he or she has learned and thinks about next steps (with input and feedback from the group).
Reflections on the process (5 min)	• The group reflects on how the process worked, and individuals share insights on what they learned.

'good' or 'well done' but has not given much detail about what makes the work good or well done." This is a description of what the person sees. In contrast, an interpretation would be to say, "This teacher isn't using any descriptive feedback, it's almost all evaluative; perhaps this is a place where he or she needs to focus." These kinds of interpretations are reserved for the third step, but it's essential that the *descriptions* are explicated first. The description step is the one that people tend to skip if left to their own devices. What tends to happen (in the absence of a protocol like this) is that the presenter tells his or her story, and then the group jumps directly to suggestion for action, without linking their interpretations to their observations. This connection between observations and interpretations is a crucial part of the process, because the description helps people make sure that they and others understand what everyone means when terms like *descriptive feedback, evaluative feedback,* or *success criteria* get bandied about.

In the fourth step, the group discusses implications for teaching and assessment, based on what they have observed and interpreted, and in the fifth step, the presenting principal summarizes what he or she has learned and uses the group to help determine where to go next, for example, how to share feedback with teachers, what to work on at his or her school's next professional learning community (PLC) meeting, etc. In the final step, the group reflects on the process, sharing their feelings about how it worked as well as what they have learned. It is essential to complete this last step every time a protocol like this is used because, remember, this process is not about the activity of "doing" the protocol; it's about using the protocol as a *tool* to help the group inquire and deepen their understanding. It's important to reflect on whether it did in fact allow for this.

We have used this example to highlight the way in which a protocol like this can help to guide an inquiry process with a group of practitioners, but there's nothing magical about this one per se. There are many different protocols out there, all with the purpose of meeting particular needs that groups of practitioners might have. Later in this chapter, we highlight another protocol for use in different circumstances—a critical friend protocol (see Table 6.2).

Making Preconceptions Explicit

Throughout this book, we've explained that one reason why it's so hard to actually learn something new (remembering that real learning is about permanent change) is because people fight very hard to hold onto existing beliefs. People don't want to *accommodate* (change their ways of thinking based on new evidence) and would prefer to *assimilate* (try to incorporate new evidence into their current ways of thinking). It's uncomfortable to question existing ways of thinking and behaving. The teacher whose understanding of persuasive writing is being challenged works very hard to hold onto her previously existing beliefs and practices about persuasive writing. The feeling of challenge is uncomfortable. And sometimes, even when it looks like there's a real change, the change is actually superficial and the person quickly reverts back to what she thought and did before once the learning encounter is over (Donovan, Bransford, & Pellegrino, 1999). For example, this same teacher whose beliefs about persuasive writing are being challenged may appear to accept her colleague's alternative perspective about persuasive writing during that actual meeting in which it's being discussed, but she may walk out of that meeting and quickly revert back to what she thought and did before.

One way to interrupt this tendency is to help people make their preconceptions explicit. Preconceptions are our beliefs, opinions, and ideas, and they are personal. Everybody carries preconceptions with them, and it's exceedingly rare—if not impossible—to find anything that a person engages with as a truly blank slate. In the case of the teacher above, preconceptions refer to what she thinks, believes, and knows about persuasive writing. And her preconceptions might be correct, partially correct, or completely erroneous. Everyone brings their already existing thoughts, feelings, and beliefs with them to any learning encounter. This is as true for adults as it is for young children.

Think about kindergarten students learning to read. Even if they've never been formally "taught" reading before, they have a multitude of previous experiences with books and with literacy in general. And think about your own experiences with professional development and professional learning. They give rise to the preconceptions that are implicated in how you engage with the ideas in this book.

Preconceptions matter; they are part of every learning encounter (often unknowingly). And typically, people don't replace them with the products of a new learning encounter. Rather, they use them to *filter* the content of the new learning encounter. Anything new that they encounter gets considered in light of their prior knowledge, and this means they have to deal with preconceptions head on; they have to know something about the nature of the filter. The kindergarten student's learning of reading is going to be filtered through the beliefs that he or she already has about literacy, and your learning from reading this book is going to be filtered through what you believed about professional learning coming in to reading it. So it is important to understand the filters, because they always work in the background and transform new learning. An important key to new learning, then, is to explicitly put preconceptions on the table and intentionally think about whether new information confirms or challenges those preconceptions. That becomes the foundation for building new knowledge.

Think of students who are learning about fractions for the first time. A very common misconception (i.e., incorrect preconception) is that a smaller fraction such as $\frac{1}{8}$ is actually greater than a bigger fraction such as $\frac{1}{4}$. The rationale for this misconception is that a student first learning about fractions already knows something (i.e., holds preconceptions) about numbers. He or she knows that 8 is bigger than 4. Given that, it's not unreasonable to assume that $\frac{1}{8}$ would be bigger than $\frac{1}{4}$. Importantly, though, what research (Donovan et al., 1999) has shown is that, if the teacher simply *tells* students that $\frac{1}{4}$ is actually greater than $\frac{1}{8}$ but does not give students the opportunity to examine their preconceptions and determine where they went wrong, it tends not to turn into real learning. What tends to happen is that students seem to "get it" in the moment—and may even regurgitate it on the test—but many ultimately revert back to their original thinking at a later time or in a different context. What looks like learning turns out not to be learning because the "permanence" criterion is missing. The act of good teaching is about getting students to make their preconceptions explicit up front (for example, by asking students probing questions about their assumptions about numbers and fractions) and then creating the conditions for students to test the fidelity of their preconceptions. That's one reason why Assessment for Learning has consistently been shown to be such a powerful pedagogy (Black & Wiliam, 1998; Hattie & Timperley, 2007); it defines teaching as a targeted response to what the teacher learns about the student's thinking from assessment.

Some people believe that their preconceptions don't matter. As one professional development participant told us, "I'm here to learn something new about Guided Reading from an expert who really knows about this. I'm throwing out what I thought and knew before and starting again." But this isn't possible. This participant can't throw out what she thought or knew before; that information will always be with her. Instead, what she needs to do is make it explicit so she can take it up, examine it, and reconcile it with new information. Learning doesn't happen by ignoring preconceptions. It happens by explicating and confronting them and by determining whether the new ideas support or challenge prior beliefs. New knowledge gets constructed by putting all that together.

One strategy that we have used to help people make their tacit knowledge explicit is to begin all formal professional learning encounters (PLC meetings, workshops, etc.) with a quick activity that gets at tacit knowledge. The specifics of the questions asked will depend on the content of the professional learning agenda, but the session begins by asking participants to privately record their beliefs about the topic (what we call "making your filters explicit"), as well as their hypotheses about what they will learn. And at the end of the session, participants are asked to consider what they heard during the session, how it related to their original preconceptions, and what they have learned. We also recommend finishing with a question about what the participant will do next based on what they've learned that day (that one's not about making preconceptions explicit, but it's still important!). As a concrete example, one secondary school that we work with has a focus on encouraging self-regulation in their students. They recently invited a well-known educational researcher in the area of self-regulation to speak to their staff. At the outset of the session, each participant was given a piece of paper and asked to answer the following questions:

1. What do I know about self-regulation?

2. Why is self-regulation important for me to know about? How does it relate to my students and to my job as a teacher? Why am I here today?

3. What do I hope to learn?

And at the end of the session, participants were handed a second sheet and asked to answer the following questions:

1. What did I hear today (a summary)?

2. How did this relate to what I thought about self-regulation before today? What was confirmatory? What was surprising?

3. Learning is about a change in the way I think. What did I learn today about self-regulation?

4. What will I do next based on what I learned today?

Ensuring That Activities and Interventions Are Rooted in Problems of Practice

One of the biases that we described in Chapter 5 involves the fact that human beings tend not to think through all the possible avenues to a problem before jumping to action. They tend to commit to decisions before considering the problem in depth, which can land them in an activity trap if it turns out that they didn't represent the problem correctly. This tendency to jump to action too quickly can also lead them to fall prey to the recognition heuristic that we described in Chapter 5 (placing greater value on things that we recognize than on things that we don't). This is because jumping to action too quickly may sometimes lead to commitment to a solution or adoption of a strategy simply because it's well known and, as a result, miss the opportunity to learn from a strategy or resource that better applies to the problem of practice. One fairly simple strategy to intentionally interrupt the human propensity to jump to action is to follow the steps of the inquiry cycle outlined in Chapter 4. The first step in the cycle is to determine what the problem of practice is and why. The "why" part necessitates that you make an evidence-based case for your problem of practice, and the activity of unpacking and describing the problem works to ensure that you represent the problem at a sufficient level of depth so as to guard against ending up in an activity trap.

We often encourage the learning communities that we work with to intentionally be on the lookout for activity traps. This is difficult, because one of the hallmarks of an activity trap is that you don't know you're in one when you're in one. The "activity trap monitor" is a brief and simple exercise designed to help school leaders (both formal and informal) determine if initiatives or activities that the school wishes to engage in may be activity traps. Every time a school (or a subgroup within it) embarks on a new "doing," we ask that they pause and explicitly answer the following four questions that essentially force them to articulate a "theory of action":

1. Briefly describe the activity/initiative we are planning to engage in.

2. How is the activity/initiative linked to our professional learning focus and our particular problem of practice? What's the rationale?

3. How do we think that engaging in this activity/initiative will deepen professional understanding such that teacher thinking and practice changes in a way that will impact on student learning?

4. What will we monitor to evaluate the hypothesis we articulated in no. 3?

When learning communities are unable to answer these questions on the front end of a new activity or initiative, it's a sign that further thinking is required before deciding to either go ahead or forgo the activity/initiative altogether.

Recruiting Contradictory Evidence

Throughout this book, we have spent quite a bit of time discussing the idea of the confirmation bias—the notion that people tend to focus on information that confirms their current beliefs rather than contradicts them. The confirmation bias is problematic from a learning perspective because it encourages assimilation (trying to incorporate new information into current ways of thinking without making any changes) rather than accommodation (actually changing ways of thinking based on the consideration of new information). And true learning that takes the form of permanent change requires accommodation. One useful strategy for intentionally interrupting the confirmation bias involves recruiting contradictory evidence. Encouraging people to consider ideas that run contrary to their own thoughts and beliefs can, in effect, set up a "shape-sorter" learning opportunity. And there are a number of practical ways to facilitate this.

In Chapter 5, we described a group of teachers we recently worked with who, as part of their PLC work, were reading and discussing a professional article. We mentioned that, when we asked the teachers to explain why they had highlighted certain passages of the article, we found that they were highlighting things that they already believed to be true and that were affirming of their existing thoughts, beliefs, and practices. As we explained, these teachers were falling prey to the confirmation bias—only paying attention to the parts of the article that supported their current ways of thinking, while essentially ignoring the parts that challenged their beliefs and practices. One fairly simple way to intentionally interrupt this bias is to have readers in a situation like this use two different colored highlighters—one for points of agreement and one for points of disagreement—and require that they use both. This simple activity forces people to pay attention not only to their own perspective but to others as well, and it encourages accommodation. (This is why activities like debates in which people are forced to argue the side of an issue that they don't agree with also work quite well for learning.)

Another useful strategy for intentionally interrupting the confirmation bias is eliminating the use of group brainstorming, at least in the way that it's typically used. This strategy may seem counterintuitive and you might be thinking, "Isn't the purpose of brainstorming to get at many different perspectives?" Although this is in fact the purpose of brainstorming (often defined as "a process undertaken by a group to solve a problem by generating a variety of possible solutions"), in reality, this tends not to be the case. In fact, recent research (Kohn & Smith, 2011) has found that group brainstorming actually suppresses creativity. Although people working in groups do usually generate as many ideas as those working alone, groups tend to engage in "fixation," in that the ideas generated in groups are far less broad than they are in people who generate ideas on their own. The early ideas constrain the breadth of subsequent ideas, and participants tend not to suggest ideas that are outside the box of what the group has already generated. We have written elsewhere (see Katz, Earl, & Ben Jaafar, 2009) about the potential pitfalls of collaborative work, including the propensity for "group think" in which people who are working together quickly settle on things that they already agree on rather than seeking to preserve and explore diversity in opinion.

It turns out that the typical form of brainstorming, where groups work together to generate solutions to a problem, is actually less effective than individuals doing a similar exercise alone (Kohn & Smith, 2011). As such, while many learning communities use brainstorming in an attempt to seek alternative perspectives, in reality, this kind of brainstorming often works to support, not interrupt, the confirmation bias. Brainstorming is more likely to generate different kinds of ideas when individuals first brainstorm on their own and generate as many solutions/ideas as they can. The group activity is then a way to "take up" each individual's ideas. What is most important is that there is a systematic way of ensuring that every person's ideas make it to the bigger list. Remember, the propensity for "group think" and conformity is high, and people will be unlikely to suggest ideas that fall outside of what others in the group have already suggested. That's why it's so important for all of the ideas from the individual work to make it into the group space for consideration, because that's where multiple perspectives—and contradictory evidence—will come from. Brainstorming in this way can thus be used to recruit contradictory evidence and intentionally interrupt the confirmation bias.

Another strategy that we find useful for recruiting contradictory evidence is to look to others who are intentionally cast in the role of *critical friends*. As the name implies, critical friends embody both the qualities of critique and of friendship. They work in the spirit of friendship, but they offer an open and honest critique of another's practice in a way that a person often can't do alone (Costa & Kallick, 1995; MacBeath, 1988). Critical friends can observe what may not be apparent to insiders, facilitate reflections on issues, ask questions, probe for justification and evidence to support perceptions, and help reformulate interpretations. Teachers may act as critical friends to one another by visiting one another's classrooms and offering a critical, though supportive, observation of practice. Administrators can act as critical friends to one another by visiting one another's schools in the same kind of fashion. And consultants can often act as critical friends to either teachers or administrators. What's important in the critical friend concept is that the appraisal is in fact honest and challenging, yet with the purpose of being supportive and with an eye toward improvement. Critical friends don't tell you what you want to hear; they offer an external perspective that thwarts you from simply seeking confirming evidence. That said, the simple presence of a critical friend doesn't guarantee receptivity to the critique; you have to *want* to know. Otherwise, you will likely push back in a way that continues to seek to preserve and conserve existing beliefs, understandings, and practices.

A few of the school districts that we have worked with have constructed situations in which principals act as critical friends to one another. They visit one another's schools with a particular purpose in mind; for example, to provide a critical, yet supportive, perspective on an area of focus in the school. A popular strategy involves administrators going on "walkthroughs" of one another's schools and then debriefing around the practices that are observed. But one of the challenges associated with these kinds of critical friend visits is that the host administrators often struggle when receiving the feedback. And in fact, they often try to preempt it. We've seen many examples of a host principal, upon returning from the walkthrough, immediately saying something like, "Before we start to debrief I just want to tell you that today probably wasn't the best day for you to be here. Halloween was yesterday, the eighth graders were on a fieldtrip earlier this morning, and one of the Grade 3 classes has a supply teacher." Now all of this is likely true, but beneath the words is a subtle psychological stance of preservation and conversation (i.e., that things in this administrator's school are fine as they are)—essentially, the confirmation bias is at work!

One strategy that we like to use to intentionally interrupt this preemptive defensiveness is what we call "agree then disagree." We tell the principals that we work with that after returning from a walkthrough, they must listen to their critical friend's feedback and then state all the reasons why the critical friend might be *right*, before beginning to defend or explain the observed practices. And where the numbers cooperate, we will often ask for there to be two critical friends visiting a host principal, who debrief with one another—uninterrupted—in the presence of the host principal, who is then asked to "agree then disagree." It makes it harder to seek refuge behind the "it's just your opinion" pillar when there are two visitors. Essentially, the host principal is forced to consider the evidence brought forth by the critical friend(s), even though it is challenging. "Agree then disagree" can be used in many different contexts; essentially, any time that someone is providing feedback to someone else. What's significant about this intentional interruption strategy is that it forces people to purposefully pay attention to perspectives other than their own.

It is possible to use explicit protocols for critical friend visits. Like the protocols we described earlier in this chapter, the purpose of using a protocol for a critical friend visit is to force people to do the things that they tend not to do naturally. An example of one such protocol is given in Table 6.2. Notice that it begins by reviewing what was observed and discussed at the last critical friend visit and what goals were set at the end of that previous visit. And the protocol ends with discussing an action plan and new goals for moving forward. But what is particularly important, given the current discussion around recruiting contradictory evidence, is that the steps outlined here force the host principal to consider the observations made by the visiting critical friend(s), even if they are contrary to what he or she believes to be true.

Viewing Mistakes as Learning Opportunities

In Chapter 5, we talked about the attitude that people tend to have toward mistakes and failures. We said that despite the fact that people often say that mistakes are a good thing and help them learn (e.g., "we learn from our mistakes"), they tend to act in ways that are incongruent with this. Tugend (2011) writes about this in the business context, explaining that, while most companies *say* that they encourage risk taking and that they recognize that mistakes are an inevitable part of tasking risks, they *act* quite contrary to this attitude by rewarding successes and penalizing failures. Moreover, what matters most— and here schools are no different than companies—is that often no one takes the time to reflect on the mistakes and learn from them in a way that directs future practice. If there is any learning at all, it's usually to not take a risk again!

In this risk-averse context, intentional interruption comes by way of shifting the focus from *outcome* to *learning*. In other words, in addition to asking if the process succeeded or failed, the even more important question becomes "What did we learn?" Teachers often talk about the value of an "error-friendly" classroom, in that errors provide windows on student thinking, thus making teaching more targeted and effective. Error-friendly schools and even districts are more likely to support professional learning. And this is more than mere lip service; it speaks to a culture of learning. The reality is that mistakes provide us with feedback, and people cannot learn without this sort

Table 6.2   Critical Friend Protocol

Protocol Step (beginning post-walkthrough)	Instructions
Review of the last visit and priorities set (5 min)	• Hosting principal reviews what he or she and the critical friend observed and discussed at the last visit and what priorities and goals were set for this one.
Introduction to the walkthrough (15 min)	• Host describes the context of the walkthrough: what classrooms will be seen, what teachers are working on, etc. • Host articulates what he or she would like the visitor to focus on. • Together, they discuss the "look-fors" to pay attention to.
Walkthrough (30 min)	
Visitor describes what he or she saw (10 min)	• Avoiding interpretation or judgment about the quality • Host remains quiet.
Interpretations of what was seen (10 min)	• Together, the host and visitor interpret the observations made by the visitor. • Host agrees before he or she disagrees.
Implications for practice (10 min)	• Based on the observations and interpretations, the host and visitor discuss implications for the host and the teachers in the school.
Planning next steps (10 min)	• Host summarizes what he or she has learned from the visit and feedback. • Host plans what he or she will do between now and the next critical friend visit (how he or she will provide feedback to the teachers and what the action plan will be). • Visitor remains a critical, yet supportive, partner in the conversation.
Planning next critical friend visit (2 min)	• This always gets done immediately, to show that continuity is a priority.
Reflect on the process (5 min)	• Both participants reflect on how the process worked and share any new insights.

of feedback. Our own work (Earl & Katz, 2006a) has found that learning from failed initiatives (either teaching initiatives or professional learning initiatives) is a better predictor of changed practice than is learning from successful initiatives. The caveat is that you have to know that you failed and that you have to think about why. There's a well-known story of a junior trader at IBM who shamefully reported to the director's office after losing $10 million of the company's money. Expecting to be fired, you can imagine his surprise when the director said, "You can't be serious. Why would we fire you now? We've just spent $10 million on your education!"

When a school has an authentic inquiry-driven learning culture, mistakes become "mis-takes." People learn from the previous "take," make revisions accordingly, and try a different "take." As we explained in Chapter 4 when we detailed the inquiry cycle, an inquiry-based methodology doesn't always yield *best practice* right out of the gate, but it does yield *next practice*. And when next practice is learning driven, it has a chance of becoming best practice.

Learning from mistakes or failures hinges on two interrelated factors. The first is actually knowing that the initiative failed, and the second is being willing to admit it. And the biases discussed in the last chapter—like illusory superiority—constrain the likelihood of both. People often don't know that an initiative failed because they don't ask; they've already moved on to the next thing. They are often so deeply embedded in a culture of activity or "doing" (as we've already talked about) that, when they finish one activity, they move onto the next before taking the time to reflect on the success (or lack thereof) of the first. People may, for instance, engage in a book study on differentiated instruction but not monitor its impact on classroom practice because, once the book study is "over," they move on to the next professional learning activity (or book). It is important to intentionally interrupt the propensity to "do" rather than to "learn."

Even if people know that an initiative failed, it's difficult to learn from it without *admitting* to its failure. Consider a teacher who undertakes a personal journey to learn about classroom assessment and then tries to make changes to her classroom practice. And imagine that she does stick with it long enough to define some success criteria and to monitor its impact on student achievement, only to find that nothing improved. Is she likely to tell anyone about it? We doubt it, given what we know about the imposter syndrome and the problematic conflation of person and practice. Practice will remain "private," and a valuable learning opportunity will be denied to the rest of the school (or division or grade). She needs to be rewarded for her learning-centeredness and risk taking in a way that's public and shapes next practice both for her and for others.

Below we show a simple sequence of questions that we have used to help schools and districts monitor the success or failure of their initiatives and to "label the learning."

1. What is the purpose of the activity or initiative?

2. What are our hypotheses about how engaging in this activity/ initiative will change teacher thinking and practice in our area of focus and subsequently impact on student achievement?

3. What are the success criteria? How will we know?

4. What evidence will speak to the success criteria?

5. What happened? What did we learn from looking at the evidence?

6. Based on what we've learned, what will we do next?

Encouraging a Growth (Rather Than a Fixed) Mindset

Exhibiting a learning orientation, as opposed to a performance orientation, and understanding mistakes as valuable learning opportunities, are manifestations of a growth mindset. The idea of growth and fixed mindsets was advanced by Carol Dweck at Stanford University through her research on achievement and success. According to Dweck (2006), people with a fixed mindset believe that their basic qualities and abilities, like intelligence, are fixed and can't be changed. These individuals believe that people either have a certain quality or ability or they don't and that this can't be developed. People with a fixed mindset tend to want to show others that they're smart and tend to avoid things that might show their deficiencies. As Dweck writes,

> Believing that your qualities are carved in stone—the fixed mindset—creates an urgency to prove yourself over and over. If people only have a certain amount of intelligence, a certain personality, and a certain moral character—well, then they'd better prove that they have a healthy dose of them. (p. 6)

In contrast, people with a growth mindset believe that basic qualities and abilities, like intelligence, can be developed through effort and hard work. These people believe that although all human beings differ in their initial abilities and skills, these things can be cultivated through effort and experience. As such, people with a growth mind-set tend to take on challenges, work hard, and confront deficiencies, because these are all about learning and improvement.

We've already talked a number of times in this book about the importance of taking risks when it comes to learning. We've also talked about how hard learning is and that it requires effort. What Dweck (2006) shows is that people's ideas about effort and risk taking are a product of their mindsets, in that people with a growth mindset are much more likely to exert effort, take risks, and focus on learning rather than performance "appearances." The important work, then, is to intentionally interrupt the fixed mindset that many of the cognitive biases we explored in the last chapter play into and, instead, encourage a growth mindset that has learning at its heart. And importantly, research (e.g., Aronson, Fried, & Good, 2002; Blackwell, Trzesniewski, & Dweck, 2007; Good, Aronson, & Inzlicht, 2003) has shown that a growth mind-set can be taught. In these studies, students (from junior high school through university) were taught that their brains form new connections through learning and that they really can become smarter. Students in these studies showed increases in motivation and/or grades (depending on the particular study) after being explicitly taught this.

In Chapter 5, where we described the cognitive biases that impede real new learning, we explained how most people consider themselves to be an exception to needing to learn anything new. And we saw, by extension, that people are pretty bad at estimating their own abilities. Dweck shows that those with a growth mindset are actually much more accurate at self-evaluation because they need accurate information about their abilities in order to learn more effectively. In contrast, since those with a fixed mindset believe that they can't alter their abilities, they are much more likely to distort them to paint a positive picture. Encouraging a growth mindset may interrupt the illusory superiority bias and support learning because it enables people to have a more accurate understanding of themselves and what they need to learn.

So how do you encourage a growth mindset? Research by Dweck and her colleagues shows that praising effort may encourage a growth mindset, whereas praising intelligence or success may encourage a fixed mindset. In a landmark study, Mueller and Dweck (1998) gave Grade 5 students some problem-solving tasks. After the first ten tasks, half of the students were praised for their intelligence ("Wow, you must be really smart at this"), and the other half of the students were praised for their effort ("Wow, you must have worked really hard"). The students were then asked what kind of tasks they wanted next—easier ones (the implication being that they would succeed and look smart) or more challenging ones (the implication being that they might not succeed, but they would learn a lot). Children were more likely to ask for the challenging tasks if they had been praised for effort and were more likely to ask for the easier tasks if they had been praised for intelligence. Praising students for their intelligence seemed to make them more likely to enter into a fixed mindset and, as such, they wanted to stick with tasks that made them look smart. It made them risk (and learning) averse. In contrast, those praised for effort seemed more likely to enter into a growth mindset. The researchers then gave very challenging tasks to all the students (both groups). Those who had previously been praised for intelligence showed decreased performance on future tasks, while those praised for effort showed increased performance on future tasks. Those praised for effort got better at the tasks! In other words, there was a positive *performance* implication for those with a growth mindset. It wasn't learning as an alternative to performance; it was learning in the service of a superior performance.

Mueller and Dweck's (1998) research shows that people who are praised for effort and hard work are more apt to take the risk of more challenging tasks in the future. Encouraging a growth mindset means shifting the focus from the outcome alone ("success" or "failure") to the outcome as understood through the process (effort and hard work). In the context of professional learning, this means that we want the "currency" of our conversations to be *learning* rather than performance. But the default assumption is that the conversation is about performance. Think about the IBM example with the $10 million: An expected performance conversation turned out to be a learning conversation. Intentional interruption is about shifting the spotlight from performance to learning. We're not saying that performance isn't important. We're saying that performance improves when learning improves, and learning is the controllable part. A learning conversation—as opposed to a performance conversation—encourages a growth mindset. You need to make explicit that the purpose of the conversation is to learn, because otherwise the biases will ensure that the default assumption is that the conversation is about performance alone.

Ensuring That Problems of Practice Are Questions That People Are Curious About

Coming up with the "right" problem of practice is often quite challenging. In Chapter 4, we described the inquiry cycle that is an integral part of collaborative inquiry that challenges thinking and practice, a key enabler of professional learning. And you might remember that we mentioned the importance of framing problems of practice as questions. We said that people are much better at pursuing an answer to a question that they are genuinely curious about than they are at just thinking through an issue. This is because curiosity stimulates a sense of urgency, motivating people to solve the problem or answer the question. In fact, recent research (vom Stumm, Hell, & Chamorro-Premuzic, 2011) has found that curiosity is a fairly strong predictor of achievement. Curiosity gives rise to motivation, which in turn gives rise to effort. And effort is a strong predictor of achievement.

A collective problem of practice needs to be something that a learning community is naturally curious about: something vexing or puzzling that directs people on a path to figuring it out because they need and want to. Human beings are naturally curious (Willingham, 2009), and problems of practice should capitalize on this curiosity. Curiosity and questions tend to go hand-in-hand, which is why problems of practice work better when framed as questions. Think about something that you're curious about. Chances are it takes the form of a question; questions are the purest form of expressed curiosity. And think of young children who are naturally curious. They are filled with questions (sometimes it feels like a bit too many!). But the process of unpacking an issue into a question requires intentional support. People often work on something without explicitly knowing why. Willingham (2009) offers one of our favorite examples of this when he talks about how so much of what children do in school assumes the pretext of a question, but that never gets explicated. He suggests that should teachers treat the formal curriculum as a body of answers to questions that students have. It is the teacher's job to help the students explicitly frame the questions that the curriculum (or rather the learning directed by it) will try to answer.

We recently worked with a PLC that was trying to frame their problem of professional practice. They explained that they wanted to look at the use of effective feedback. Acting as critical friends to the group, we pushed them to talk about the issue in order to turn it into an inquiry question; something they wanted to be able to answer. They continued to talk about how they needed to learn about using effective feedback, and we continued to say, "But why? What's your question?" We asked a number of probing questions to get at their hypotheses—what they thought and why. After about an hour, they ended up with a refined question, but it turned out it wasn't really about feedback; it was about what makes an effective PLC. Their hypothesis was that giving and receiving effective feedback is evidence of an effective PLC, but that wasn't in and of itself the actual question that they were curious about. Pinpointing the area of curiosity is crucial because it turns on the motivation faucet. And when you're motivated to pursue an answer, you're well on your way to learning.

Giving People Autonomy in Task and Time

In his well-known book *Drive*, Daniel Pink (2009) writes about the relationship between autonomy and performance, citing evidence that people who are given freedom to work under autonomous conditions tend to be higher performing than those who are not. Importantly, Pink is clear that *autonomy* does not simply mean *independence* (working on something alone with no help from anyone else) but actually means *acting with choice*—meaning that someone can be autonomous but still collaborative. Since people who are given autonomy in their work are acting with choice, they become motivated by the inherent satisfaction that comes from what they are doing (intrinsic motivation), which leads to higher performance.

Pink writes about two specific aspects of autonomy that we consider to be especially important for the argument we're making in this book. The first is autonomy in task, which refers to giving people some choice over what they are working on (or in our case, what they are learning about). This shouldn't be taken to mean complete carte blanche; the needs-based requirement in establishing focus, as a key enabler of knowledge creation, is still there. Rather, it means that, within the needs-based requirement of a focus (remember, from student learning need to teacher learning need to leader learning need), educators should choose a problem of practice that they are curious about. Recall the point we made in the last section of this chapter: "curiosity stimulates motivation." One principal that we know believes very strongly in this notion of autonomy in task. In her school, instead of having a large-group PLC, she has a number of smaller PLCs that are teacher directed. Through a facilitated process, teachers come up with inquiry questions within the school's area of focus. They then "apply" to the principal for permission to work on their problem of practice and are given appropriate support and release time to do so. The application requires them to articulate what they're curious about and why, the evidence of the link to student needs, what they will do with their support and release time, and how they will know if it's made a difference (in essence, the major components of the inquiry cycle described in Chapter 4). And the principal uses back and forth revisions of the application as an opportunity to act as a critical friend and help the group refine their inquiry question. This process ensures that teachers are given some autonomy in task but it is a facilitated process that keeps the group within the school's area of focus and out of activity traps.

Related to autonomy in task is the notion of autonomy in time. Pink (2009) references research suggesting that, if you want people to do good work, then you should let them focus on the work, not on the time it takes to complete it. His argument is that for many tasks, particularly those that aren't predictable (like the problems of practice we've been taking about), the time it takes to complete something and what gets produced don't have an obvious connection. As we noted at the beginning of this book, the biggest obstacle that both teachers and leaders tend to cite in terms of professional learning in schools is time. People tend to say, "If only we had more time, we could do . . ." However, when the problem of practice is sufficiently motivating, the focus tends to move from the time to the actual work. And that produces results. Consider, for example, a teacher who is working hard to learn about critical thinking. It's a Saturday morning, and this teacher has stopped by her local bookstore to pick up the weekly entertainment magazines that she likes to read on the weekends. While she's there, she notices a new book on critical thinking and stops to flip through it. This teacher isn't saying, "There's no way I'm looking at that on my weekend. It's work!" If she's anything like some of incredible teachers we know, she buys the book (with her own money), publicly exclaims how she can't believe what a lucky find it was, and might even start reading it before the entertainment magazines that very weekend. When a task is sufficiently motivating, the challenge of time tends to move to the background, and the time problem often takes care of itself. This really highlights the importance of what we've been saying in both this section and the previous one; problems of practice that are authentic, needs based, and rooted in curiosity are much more motivating to work on. And this makes learning more likely and interference from the biases less likely.

Moving Forward

In Chapter 4, we described three key enablers of real professional learning: focus, collaborative inquiry that challenges thinking and practice, and instructional leadership (formal and informal). In Chapter 5, we described the impediments to implementation of the enablers in terms of the cognitive biases that inhibit real new learning—that permanent change in thinking or behavior. And in this chapter, we've outlined eight strategies that can work to intentionally interrupt the biases, thus allowing professional learning (of the real sort) to be enabled:

1. Using protocols

2. Making preconceptions explicit

3. Ensuring that activities and interventions are rooted in problems of practice

4. Recruiting contradictory evidence

5. Viewing mistakes as learning opportunities

6. Encouraging a growth (rather than a fixed) mindset

7. Ensuring that problems of practice are questions that people are curious about

8. Giving people autonomy in time and task

Having read this far, you are already on your way to enabling real professional learning. Why would that be? Because we know that awareness is the first step in intentional interruption. The biases work silently in the background, often beneath conscious awareness, but consistently thwarting implementation of the key enablers of real professional learning. You now know about the biases, about how they work, and about how to intentionally interrupt so as to minimize their impact. Awareness is an important first step. But it's not enough.

The Importance of Knowing AND Doing

Well-established research (Donovan et al., 1999) has shown that one of the most important components of how people learn is *metacognition*. Metacognition refers to a person's knowledge about his or her own cognitive processes (Flavell, 1976), or more casually, it means thinking about one's own thinking or learning. Importantly, there are two components of metacognition. The first is "knowing" and the second is "doing," or "regulation." It's not enough for people to *know* themselves; that's why awareness is only a first step. They must also *monitor* themselves. The challenge with metacognition often lies in the monitoring part. For example, a teacher who takes part in a PLC meeting focused on backward design might be well aware that if she doesn't try to put some of what she's learned into place in her classroom fairly quickly after that meeting, she'll be unlikely to ever get back to it. That's the "knowing" part. The "regulation" part or question is, does she actually do that? People often know what they *should* do, but still have trouble actually doing it.

The reason we're mentioning this is that the same idea applies to the notion of intentional interruption. Awareness of what needs to be interrupted and how to intentionally interrupt is a necessary first step. But the learning power is in the regulation: actually doing it. This book has hopefully provided you with the awareness (or the knowing) piece by helping you build an understanding of what needs to be in place for true professional learning to happen, the barriers that might get in the way, and strategies for interrupting these barriers. The next step is where you regulate your behavior and actually put what you know into action. The first step in doing that is to start right away.

Don't Wait, Start Now!

Whether you're a principal, a teacher, a consultant, or a district administrator, if you're reading this book, you're probably already involved in some kind of a professional learning environment. You're likely not starting from scratch at this point. And you shouldn't want to. We are not suggesting that you abandon all professional learning plans and activities that you are currently involved in and start over. We're suggesting that you work from wherever you are. We hope you now have an image of what real professional learning can look like, but you don't need a blank slate to make it a reality. In fact, we wouldn't recommend starting from scratch for a couple of reasons.

First, it is possible to get so caught up in trying to build a PLC that's "ready" to start working that you never get to the part where the real work (i.e., the learning—the *L* in PLC) happens. It's like the well-known correlation between perfectionism and procrastination. Perfectionists are so concerned with getting it right that they avoid starting. We've worked with several principals who regularly say that the teachers in their schools aren't "ready" to start working together in meaningful ways because they haven't yet developed a robust sense of professional trust. This is problematic because trust is more of a product of collaborative encounters than a prerequisite for them (Katz et al., 2009). A minimal amount of relational trust is important so that people are willing to "take a chance" together. If they wait for more than that, they'll likely be waiting forever.

Second, and perhaps even more important from our perspective, is understanding that most of the barriers to real new learning that we described in the previous chapter can't be preempted, even with the most intentionally constructed professional learning environment. The biases are an innate and integral part of human nature. At many levels—albeit not always learning ones—they're functional. That's why we talk about interrupting them instead of preventing them. The biases are also not purely cognitive but rather a complex interplay between cognition and emotion; elements of both head and heart comingle. Neuroscience helps us understand this relationship. In our brains, the prefrontal cortex controls conscious thought, while the amygdala is the source of our emotions. And the amygdala is much more primitive as a neural structure, so we tend to feel things a lot faster than we think them. Trying to preempt emotion with cognition doesn't really work. You can't, for example, tell someone not to feel like an imposter (remember the imposter syndrome). What you can do, however, is tell someone that you know that at some point in the process they will feel like an imposter and that, when that unavoidable feeling arises, there are ways to respond to it and make sense of it, such that the impact is reduced (i.e., interrupt—not preempt—the emotion). So, take the pressure off yourself. You aren't starting from scratch. Work with what you have and respond to your reality in ways that will shape the direction of professional learning. That's what interruption is all about. Interruption is about intentionally responding to the biases that impede real new learning.

Time for Reflection

Think through the following questions:

- In the reflection questions at the end of Chapter 1, we asked whether you consider yourself a facilitator of professional learning. Revisit your initial answer to that question. Having read the rest of the book, how might your answer change?
- This book finished with a section called, "Don't Wait, Start Now!" What are some specific actions that you are going to take to move forward with your professional learning efforts?
- This chapter has presented an array of tools for intentional interruption. We discussed the importance of using tools in a fit-for-purpose way, by starting with the need and then choosing a relevant tool. What do you see as your most urgent professional learning "interruption need," and which tool might best meet that need?

References

Aronson, J., Fried, C. B., & Good, C. (2002). Reducing the effects of stereotype threat on African American college students by shaping theories of intelligence. *Journal of Experimental Social Psychology, 38,* 113–125.

Assessment Reform Group. (2002). *Assessment is for learning: 10 principles.* Retrieved January 14, 2010, from http://assessmentreformgroup.files .wordpress.com/2012/01/10principles_english.pdf

Black, P., & Wiliam, D. (1998). Inside the black box: Raising standards through classroom assessment. *Phi Delta Kappan, 80,* 139–148.

Blackwell, L., Trzesniewski, K., & Dweck, C. S. (2007). Implicit theories of intelligence predict achievement across an adolescent transition: A longitudinal study and an intervention. *Child Development, 78,* 246–263.

Borko, H., & Putnam, R. (1996). Learning to teach. In R. C. Calfee & D. C. Berliner (Eds.), *Handbook of educational psychology* (pp. 673–708). New York, NY: Macmillan.

Bucciarelli, M., & Johnson-Laird, P. N. (2001). Falsification and the role of the theory of mind in the reduced array selection task. *Current Psychology Letters, 4,* 7–22.

Costa, A., & Kallick, B. (1995). Through the lens of a critical friend. In A. Costa and B. Kallick (Eds.), *Assessment in the learning organization: Shifting the paradigm* (pp. 153–156). Alexandria, VA: Association for Supervision and Curriculum Development.

Crooks, T. (1988). The impact of classroom evaluation practices on students. *Review of Educational Research, 58*(4), 438–481.

Cummins, D. D. (1996). Evidence of deontic reasoning in 3- and 4-year-old children. *Memory and Cognition, 24,* 823–829.

Dack, L. A. (2008). Deontic and epistemic reasoning in children. *Dissertation Abstracts International: Section B: The Sciences and Engineering, 69,* 12-B.

Darling-Hammond, L. (2000). Teacher quality and student achievement: A review of state policy evidence. *Educational Policy Analysis Archives.* Retrieved from http://epaa.asu.edu/epaa/v8n1

Dattner, B., & Dahl, D. (2011). *The blame game: How the hidden rules of credit and blame determine our success or failure.* New York, NY: Free Press.

Donovan, M. S., Bransford, J. D., & Pellegrino, J. W. (1999). *How people learn: Bridging research and practice.* Commission on Behavioral and Social Sciences and Education. Washington, DC: National Academy Press.

Dweck, C. S. (2006). *Mindset: The new psychology of success.* New York, NY: Random House.

Earl, L., & Katz, S. (2006a). How networked learning communities work. *Centre for Strategic Education Seminar Series Paper, 155,* 1–20.

Earl, L., & Katz, S. (2006b). *Rethinking classroom assessment with a purpose in mind.* Western and Northern Canadian Protocol for Collaboration in Education. Retrieved June 30, 2011, from www.edu.gov.mb.ca/k12/assess/wncp/index.html

Earl, L., Volante, L., & Katz, S. (2011). Understanding assessment for learning: What does it take to unleash its promise? *Education Canada, 51,* 17–20.

Easton, L. B. (2009). *Protocols for professional learning.* Alexandria, VA: ASCD.

Elmore, R. F. (1996). Getting to scale with good educational practice. *Harvard Educational Review, 66,* 1–26.

Elmore, R. (2007). Professional networks and school improvement. *School Administrator, 64,* 20–24.

Evans, J. St. B. T., & Feeney, A. (2004). The role of prior belief in reasoning. In J. P. Leighton & R. J. Sternberg (Eds.), *The nature of reasoning* (pp. 78–102). New York, NY: Cambridge University Press.

Flavell, J. H. (1976). Metacognitive aspects of problem solving. In L. B. Resnick (Ed.), *The nature of intelligence* (pp. 231–235). Hillsdale, NJ: Erlbaum.

Gilbert, D. T. (2006). *Stumbling on happiness.* New York, NY: Alfred A. Knopf.

Glaser, R., & Chi, M. (1988). Introduction: What is it to be an expert? In M. Chi, R. Glaser, & M. Farr (Eds.), *The nature of expertise.* Hillsdale, NJ: Erlbaum.

Good, C., Aronson, J., & Inzlicht, M. (2003). Improving adolescents' standardized test performance: An intervention to reduce the effects of stereotype threat. *Applied Developmental Psychology, 24,* 645–662.

Gregory, G. H., & Kuzmich, L. (2007). *Teacher teams that get results: 61 strategies for sustaining and renewing professional learning communities.* Thousand Oaks, CA: Corwin.

Guskey, T. R. (2000). *Evaluating professional development.* Thousand Oaks, CA: Corwin.

Hakkarainen, K., Palonen, T., Paavola, S., & Lehtinen, E. (2004). *Communities of networked expertise: Professional and educational perspectives.* Amsterdam, The Netherlands: Elsevier.

Hatano, G., & Oura, Y. (2003). Reconceptualising school learning using insight from expertise research. *Educational Researcher, 32,* 26–29.

Hattie, J. (2009). *Visible learning.* Abingdon, UK: Routledge.

Hattie, J., & Timperley, H. (2007). The power of feedback. *Review of Educational Research, 77,* 81–112.

Hord, S. M., & Sommers, W. A. (2008). *Leading professional learning communities: Voices from research and practice.* Thousand Oaks, CA: Corwin.

Jackson, D., & Temperley, J. (2006, January). From professional learning community to networked learning community. Paper presented at the

International Conference of School Effectiveness and Improvement, Fort Lauderdale, FL.

James, M., & Pedder, D. (2006). Beyond method: Assessment and learning practices and values. *The Curriculum Journal, 17*, 109–138.

Kaagan, S. S., & Headley, L. (2010). *Bringing your learning community to life: A roadmap for sustainable school improvement.* Thousand Oaks, CA: Corwin.

Katz, S., & Dack, L. A. (2009). A learning network implementation study: The case of the GAPPRS networked learning community. Research report for the District School Board of Niagara. St. Catherine's, ON, Canada: Aporia Consulting Ltd.

Katz, S., Dack, L. A., & Earl, L. (2009). Networked learning communities to foster learning for teachers and their students. *Principal Connections, 12*, 36–38.

Katz, S., & Earl, L. (2005). *Research report: Classroom assessment.* Ontario, Canada: Greater Toronto Area Professional Network Centre.

Katz, S., & Earl, L. M. (2010). Learning about networked learning communities. *School Effectiveness and School Improvement, 21*, 27–51.

Katz, S., Earl, L., & Ben Jaafar, S. (2009). *Building and connecting learning communities: The power of networks for school improvement.* Thousand Oaks, CA: Corwin.

Kohn, N. W., & Smith, S. M. (2011). Collaborative fixation: Effects of others' ideas on brainstorming. *Applied Cognitive Psychology, 25*, 359–371.

Learning. (n.d.). In *Dictionary.com.* Retrieved July 15, 2011, from http://www.dictionary.reference.com/browse/learning

Learning. (n.d.). In *Wikipedia: The free encyclopedia.* Retrieved July 15, 2011, from http://www.en.wikipedia.org/wiki/Learning

Learning. (n.d.). In *WordNet search.* Retrieved July 15, 2011, from http://wordnetweb.princeton.edu/perl/webwn?s=learning&sub=Search+WordNet&o2=&o0=1&o8=1&o1=1&o7=&o5=&o9=&o6=&o3=&o4=&h=

Legrenzi, P., Girotto, V., & Johnson-Laird, P. N. (1993). Focusing in reasoning and decision making. *Cognition, 49*, 37–66.

Levesque, H. J. (1989). Logic and the complexity of reasoning. In R. H. Thomason (Ed.), *Philosophical logic and artificial intelligence* (pp. 73–107). Dordrecht, The Netherlands: Kluwer Academic Publishers.

Levin, B. (2011). Achieving equity through innovation: A Canada–U.S. dialogue. *Education Canada, 51*, 19–21.

Little, J. W. (1990). The persistence of privacy: Autonomy and initiative in teachers' professional relations. *Teachers College Record, 91*, 509–536.

Little, J. W., & Curry, M. (2008). Structuring talk about teaching and learning: The use of evidence in protocol-based conversation. In L. Earl and H. Timperley (Eds.), *Professional learning conversations: Challenges in using evidence for improvement* (pp. 29–42). UK: Springer.

Louis, K. S., Leithwood, K., Wahlstrom, K. L., Anderson, S. E. (2010). Learning from leadership: Investigating the links to improved student learning. Retrieved from http://www.wallacefoundation.org/knowledge-center/school-leadership/key-research/Documents/Investigating-the-Links-to-Improved-Student-Learning.pdf

MacBeath, J. (1988). "I didn't know he was ill": The role and value of the critical friend. In L. Stoll & K. Myers (Eds.), *No quick fixes: Perspectives on school in difficulty* (pp. 118–132). London, UK: Falmer Press.

Marzano, R. J. (2003). *What works in schools: Translating research into action.* Alexandria, VA: Association for Supervision and Curriculum Development.

Marzano, R., Pickering, D., & Pollock, J. (2001). *Classroom instruction that works: Research-based strategies for increasing student achievement.* Alexandria, VA: Association for Supervision and Curriculum Development.

McDonald, J., Mohr, N., Dichter, A., & McDonald, E. (2007). *The power of protocols: An educator's guide to better practice.* New York, NY: Teachers College Press.

Mueller, C. M., & Dweck, C. S. (1998). Praise for intelligence can undermine children's motivation and performance. *Journal for Personality and Social Psychology, 75,* 33–52.

Muijs, D., West, M., & Ainscow, M. (2010). Why network? Theoretical perspectives on networking. *School Effectiveness and School Improvement, 21,* 5–26.

National Institute of Health. (n.d.). *The brain: Our sense of self.* Retrieved July 15, 2011, from http://www.science.education.nih.gov/supplements/ nih4/Self/other/glossary.htm

Nelson, T. H., Slavit, D., Perkins, M., & Hathorn, T. (2008). A culture of collaborative inquiry: Learning to develop and support professional learning communities. *Teachers College Record, 110,* 1269–1303.

Nye, B., Konstantanopooulos, S., & Hedges, L. (2004). How large are teacher effects? *Educational Evaluation and Policy Analysis, 26,* 237–257.

Olson, D. R., & Katz, S. (2001). The fourth folk pedagogy. In B. Torff & R. J. Sternberg (Eds.), *Understanding and teaching the intuitive mind* (pp. 243–263), New Jersey, NJ: Lawrence Erlbaum Associates, Inc.

Passer, M., Smith, R., Atkinson, M., Mitchell, J., & Muir, D. (2005). *Psychology frontiers and applications* (2nd Canadian ed.). Toronto, Canada: McGraw-Hill Ryerson.

Piaget, J. (1952). *The origins of intelligence in children.* New York, NY: International Universities Press. (Original work published 1936)

Pink, D. H. (2009). *Drive: The surprising truth about what motivates us.* New York, NY: Riverhead Books.

Popham, J. (2011). Formative assessment—A process, not a test. Published Online: February 22, 2011 Education Week. Retrieved from http://www .edweek.org/ew/articles/2011/02/23/21popham.h30.html

Pronin, E. (2006). Perception and misperception of bias in human judgment. *Trends in Cognitive Sciences, 11,* 37–43.

Psychology. (n.d.). In *The free dictionary.* Retrieved July 15, 2011, from http:// www.thefreedictionary.com/psychology

Resolve: The National Infertility Association. (n.d.). Myths and Facts About Infertility. Retrieved September 1, 2011, from http://www.resolve.org/ support-and-services/for-family--friends/myths-and-facts.html

Ritov, I., & Baron, J. (1990). Reluctance to vaccinate: Omission bias and ambiguity. *Journal of Behavioral Decision Making, 3,* 263–277.

Roberts, S. M., & Pruitt, E. Z. (2009). *Schools as professional learning communities: Collaborative activities and strategies for professional development* (2nd ed.). Thousand Oaks, CA: Corwin.

Robinson, V., Höhepa, M., & Lloyd, C. (2009). *School leadership and student outcomes: Identifying what works and why: A best evidence synthesis.* Wellington, New Zealand: Ministry of Education.

Sanders, W. L., & Horn, S. P. (1994). The Tennessee value-added assessment system (TVAAS): Mixed-model methodology in educational assessment. *Journal of Personnel Evaluation in Education, 8,* 299–311.

Shafir, E. (1994). Uncertainty and the difficulty of thinking through disjunctions. *Cognition, 50,* 403–430.

Spillane, J. (2006). *Distributed leadership.* San Francisco, CA: Jossey-Bass.

Stanovich, K. E. (2009). *What intelligence tests miss: The psychology of rational thought.* New Haven, CT: Yale University Press.

Sullivan, P. (2010). *Clutch: Why some people excel under pressure and others don't.* New York, NY: Penguin Group.

Supovitz, J. (2006). *The case for district-based reform: Leading, building, and sustaining school improvement.* Cambridge, MA: Harvard University Press.

Timperley, H. S. (2011). *Realizing the power of professional learning.* London, UK: Open University Press.

Toplak, M. E., & Stanovich, K. E. (2002). The domain specificity and generality of disjunctive reasoning: Searching for a generalizable critical thinking skill. *Journal of Educational Psychology, 94,* 197–209.

Tugend, A. (2011). *Better by mistake: The unexpected benefits of being wrong.* New York, NY: Penguin Group.

vom Stumm, S., Hell, B., & Chamorro-Premuzic, T. (2011). The hungry mind: Intellectual curiosity is the third pillar of academic performance. *Perspectives on Psychological Science, 6,* 574–588.

Wallace, M. R. (2009). Making sense of the links: Professional development, teacher practices, and student achievement. *Teachers College Record, 111,* 573–596.

Wansink, B. (Interview with; 2011, May). Under the influence: How external cues make us overeat. *Nutrition Action Healthletter,* 3–7.

Wason, P. C. (1966). Reasoning. In B. M. Foss (Ed.), *New horizons in psychology* (Vol. 1). Harmandsworth, UK: Penguin.

Willingham, D. T. (2009). *Why don't students like school?* San Francisco, CA: Jossey-Bass.

Woolfolk, A., Winne, P., & Perry, N. (2012). *Educational psychology* (5th Canadian ed.). Toronto, Canada: Pearson.

Wright, S. P., Horn, S. P., & Sanders, W. L. (1997). Teacher and classroom context effects on student achievement: Implications for teacher evaluation. *Journal of Personnel Evaluation in Education, 11,* 57–67.

Index